Dad Was an Artist

A Survivor's Story

J. Jason Horejs

Edited by Karly Williams

Cover photo: Devon Horejs

Put Your Handkerchief Away—
This Isn't One of Those Stories

The bookstore is full of memoirs by writers who grew up in heartbreaking conditions. If all one had to go by were these autobiographical tragedies, one might think that all parents are alcoholics, and that every child grows up in grinding poverty, abused and neglected.

Mine is not one of those stories, and this is not one of those books. Even as a small child, I knew that I was pretty lucky. I grew up in a house where my parents loved each other, and loved me and my siblings. My sisters and brothers were my best friends. My family went on adventures, read books together, and spent a lot of time laughing.

Looking back now, it's not hard to see that my childhood was idyllic in many ways.

Oh sure, my dad, a fine artist, had chosen one of the most unlikely of careers in the small, agricultural town in Southern Idaho where I grew up. And yes, there were long stretches where we didn't have any money. Perhaps we did reside in fairly unusual habitations as my parents pursued utopian visions. And, alright, my dad did end up in the federal penitentiary, and my mother on supervised probation.

But other than that, my childhood was pretty unremarkable.

1

HOREJS

We might as well get this out of the way now. My last name is Horejs. The reader will be best served by skipping over the name whenever it pops up. The way it's pronounced has very little to do with the way it's spelled, and so even though I'm going to provide pronunciation guidance now, I know that seeing the name in print completely erases any confidence the reader might feel when required to articulate the name.

The name is Czech in origin, and apparently Eastern Europeans don't believe in vowels, or perhaps my ancestors were too poor to afford any.

Actually, my great, great grandfather, John Joseph Horejsie (1850-1902), who was born in the Bohemian region of what is now the Czech Republic, had his fair share of vowels. In fact, he had one more than his father, who spelled the name "Horejsi."

Somewhere between John Joseph's birth in Czechoslovakia and his death in Iowa, we lost the "ie", and my great grandfather was born Frank Horejs in 1893. I like to tell the story that the name was shortened on the chopping block of the register on Ellis Island, when officials decided that the name was too much of a mess, but I can't find any evidence that this is actually what occurred.

When I was a kid, family lore maintained that the name meant "highborn", and I became convinced that my ancestors were Czech royalty. I expected that someday an attorney would appear to announce that as the first born of a first born of a first born (and so on), I was heir to a vast fortune. It didn't seem that far-fetched then; after all, most of my friends had last names like "Holt", "Hanks", or "Bell", names about as rare as potatoes in Idaho. I didn't know anyone who had my last name.

When my parents eventually took a trip to the Czech Republic with my grandparents in the 1990s, they discovered that the cemeteries were filled with Horejsis, Horejsies, and other variations of the name. The name was about as rare as "Smith" or "Jones".

My genealogical research has revealed that Horejs does indeed mean "high born"—as in, the family lived in the upper part of the village.

Oh well.

And so, without further ado, the best way to pronounce the name is with an "sh" sound at the end. "Horsh", rhyming with Porsche, unless one is pretentious and pronounces the final "e" in Porsche with an accent, like the Germans do . . .

As I said, you're better off skipping over it.

The Setting

Burley, Idaho is, and has been, as long as I have known it, a town in decline. With a population of about 8,000 when I was growing up there, and only 10,000 or so thirty years later, it's clear that the growth brought to other parts of the state as Californians have moved there has mostly avoided Burley.

As in many small American towns, the main thoroughfare, Overland Ave, is lined with empty storefronts and a hodgepodge of mom and pop shops and cafes. Occasionally there will be a newer building that springs up to house a dental office or chiropractor, but most of the buildings saw their heyday in the 1930s, '40s, or '50s. It's all been downhill since then.

Situated on a bend in the Snake River, Burley is home to potato, sugar beet, and corn farmers, and to the people who sell stuff to the farmers. Everything in town revolves around the planting, cultivating, and harvesting seasons.

Burley was settled by Mormon pioneers, as were many of the other towns in the area. Because it was fortunate enough to be positioned on a mainline of the railroad, it turned out to be one of the larger settlements. The town was named after David Ellsworth Burley, a railroad official. The first post office in town made its appearance in 1905, and I recall learning in grade school that Burley was incorporated in 1910 (a date I remember only because it happened to be the same year Halley's comet made a celestial visit, an event that interested me quite a bit).

Idaho is a scenic state with a varied topography. The Sawtooth Mountains in Central Idaho, with their exposed granite peaks, rival the Tetons in beauty, and surpass them in remoteness and solitude. Vast pine forests cover much of the state, and the panhandle in the north is home to breathtakingly beautiful lakes and rolling hills.

Southern Idaho, however, is a flat, windswept, high-country desert. Were it not for the industry of early pioneers and their labor to dam the Snake River, and spread a network of irrigation canals and ditches, the country would be a barren wasteland of sagebrush and weeds.

This is not to say that the country is unappealing. Quite the opposite. The clean, clear air of the vast open countryside allows one to see hundreds of miles in any direction. Montana might be Big Sky Country, but the heavens of Southern Idaho arguably deserve the same appellation. On particularly clear days, one can see the perennially snow-capped peaks of the Sawtooths over a hundred miles away. The countryside rolls with slight hills and dales, almost wave-like, producing a perception that the curvature of the globe can be viewed in the distance.

While I was not actually born in Burley, my parents, both Idaho natives, moved back to the area when I was just over a year old. My first memories come into focus in this landscape, and it is on this stage that the events of my early life unfold.

The Cast

My dad, John Horejs, was born in Twin Falls, a city four or five times as big as Burley, and about twenty-five miles west on the Snake.[1] His father was a World War II veteran of the Pacific War, and a fire captain in the Twin Falls Fire Department. His mother was a school teacher.

My grandparents were stern, as many children of the Great Depression were. I've heard many stories that lead me to believe that my grandfather's discipline might even have gone a step or two beyond stern. The rod was certainly not spared on my dad and his four siblings.

I myself witnessed some of that discipline growing up, when I stayed at my grandparents' home; however, my grandfather's temper seemed to mellow with time. Though I have many fond memories of time spent with my grandparents, and I know that my dad holds warm feelings toward them, I was always somewhat afraid of the man. More important for my story, for all that, is the fact that my

---

[1] Locals don't bother to add the "River"—if there's an article preceding it, you know they're not talking about a serpent.

father inherited much of my grandfather's work ethic, along with a dose of his temper—as we will see.

Grandma was sweet and loving, and sometimes just a tad kooky. Many of her grandchildren remember strange meals comprising odd combinations of ingredients. She was famous for her "funky punch", for which any variety of juices might be mixed with any variety of sodas. Dad inherited my grandmother's kindness, along with her peculiarly unique ways of putting things together.

My mother, Elaine Summers, was born in Rupert, Idaho, a town even smaller than Burley, and just a few minutes drive eastward. My Grandpa Summers was a serial entrepreneur, who at various times sold insurance, had a camper trailer dealership, was a motivational time management speaker, and had a newspaper distribution company.

Grandpa was an avid and expressive storyteller. Salesmanship and motivational speaking weren't just jobs for the man: they were his life's vocation. Grandpa loved to share anecdotes and tell jokes, though he, too, had a bit of a temper. He spoke in a crisp tenor voice that would drop almost to a baritone when he was irritated.

When he wasn't selling things or telling stories, Grandpa employed his voice singing in barbershop quartets. He read two newspapers from cover to cover every day, and was a classic film buff. When asked about any movie made between 1935 and 1960 and beyond, he could identify the stars and summarize the plot; in the case of a musical, he could sing most any song from the film.

Mom's mother was a complete opposite, and in many ways, a perfect complement to my grandfather. If he was boisterous and gregarious, she was quiet and demure. Grandma Summers had been orphaned as a young girl, when both of her parents passed away within several years of one another.

After losing her parents, Grandma grew up in the household of an acerbic aunt. It is probably indicative how she felt about her home situation that she married my grandfather within weeks of finishing high school. She was seventeen and my grandfather was eighteen.

Grandma spent most of her adult life as a bookkeeper for the Clover Club potato chip company, which meant that chips were always plentiful when we went to visit. She was a cola addict, and Tab was her caffeine-delivery beverage of choice. She was obsessed with making sure the people around her had what they needed, and were happy and content. A veritable whirlwind in the kitchen, Grandma would deftly season and prepare a fried chicken or a beef roast, peel and mash potatoes, and heat vegetables, all while her rolls rose and baked in the oven, and her pies cooled on the counter, filling the home with mouth-watering aromas.

The vegetables on the table came from Grandma's large garden, which she planted in the spring, tended and weeded through the summer, and harvested in the fall. Her home-canned produce filled many pantry shelves. Try as I might, I can't remember Grandma ever sitting still for long. She was, however, always the first to bed, early in the evening—her constant motion and activity having exhausted her.

A few paragraphs hardly do justice to my grandparents—they were all incredible in their unique ways. While distilling their lives into a few sentences falls woefully short of capturing their essences, it does serve to highlight qualities and attributes that were combined and passed to formulate my parents' characters and outlooks on life.

Mom and Dad met in the spring of 1972 when they starred opposite one another in the amateur theatrical production, *But Albert, You Promised!* I am certain the brief comedy was every bit as cheesy and corny as the title would suggest, but the romantic interest portrayed on the stage sparked an authentic attraction between the leads, and somehow, my dad, a very shy twenty-three-year-old, managed to work up the courage to ask my mother, a still-in-high-school seventeen-year-old, out on a date. I can't imagine that Mom's parents would have been able to complain too much about my parents' difference in ages, since Grandma had been practically a child bride; however, my parents leveraged some confusion around the fact that my dad had a younger brother, who was much closer in age to my mother. By the time my grandparents figured out the mistake, it was too late—the die was cast, and my parents had become engaged.

Mom moved to Provo, Utah, to attend Brigham Young University, where she lived with friends for a semester. She and my dad were married just after finals, on December 21st, 1973, which they would always embarrassingly point out was the winter solstice: the longest night of the year. After the wedding, Dad joined Mom in Provo, where he, too, became a student at BYU. Mom studied early childhood education, and Dad signed up for art courses.

Dad isn't one of those artists who can say, "I always knew I wanted to be an artist." Sure, he enjoyed drawing as a child, and was in frequent trouble in school for doodling and daydreaming, but the thought of becoming "an artist" never crossed his mind. As a matter of fact, after graduating from Twin Falls High School, Dad toyed with the idea of studying psychiatry, before ultimately enrolling in a technical course to learn how to operate computers. This was in the early days of the advent of computing machines, and he was learning how to use punch cards to process calculations.

Those who know my father today would find it difficult to imagine professions more ill-suited to my father's disposition and talents than psychiatry or computing—especially computing! I can't remember ever seeing my dad use the family's computer when I was growing up, and even today, in the height of the internet and mobile computing age, he is a reluctant and infrequent visitor to the digital world.

Instead of seeking a job after completing the computing course, Dad volunteered to serve a two year mission for The Church of Jesus Christ of Latter-day Saints. I say "volunteered", but Mormon young men are practically compelled to serve. My grandfather was a convert to the faith, and didn't pressure his son to sign up. In fact, when he agreed to fund my dad's computer course, he informed him that if he paid for the class, he wouldn't be interested in also funding a mission.[2] However, when the time came, and my father was assigned to learn French and spread the Gospel in France, my grandfather had a change of heart and agreed to also pay for the mission.

While serving in France, Dad learned to speak French fluently—so fluently, in fact, that to this day, over forty years after his mission, French tourists are quick to compliment him on his accent. This never fails to impress me, because I know the French are notoriously hard to please!

When he returned from his mission, Dad took a job at Sears Roebuck, and drifted as he tried to determine a direction in his life. It was at this point that a fateful invitation came from his Aunt Barbara, his mother's sister, who was as sweet an aunt as one could ever imagine.

Aunt Barbara was an amateur painter, and she invited my dad to join her for a day of painting. That invitation changed the course of his life, and for better and worse, set my dad on the path to becoming a professional fine artist. There was

---

[2] Many people mistakenly think that Mormon missionaries are paid for their proselytizing. Not only are they not remunerated, the missionary and his family pay for all of the expenses incurred while serving.

something about laying the oil paint on the canvas that captured my father's imagination.

Even as he was caught up in the magic of painting, I'm not sure Dad felt that painting could eventually become a career. It was unlikely that he had seen any examples of artists who had successfully turned their artistic passions into paying vocations.

If one were to visualize a hub of the fine art universe, a mecca of creativity where art was encouraged and appreciated, Southern Idaho would be at the point most distant from that hub. It's difficult to imagine a population more immune to creativity and artistic invention than that comprised of the farmers, merchants, and tractor salesmen of Idaho.

There certainly was no "art scene", and the nearest galleries were in Boise and Sun Valley, several hours drive and a world away from the towns in which my parents had grown up. While there were art classes at the high school and the community college, the highest aspiration of the typical art student in the area was to pass the class, or perhaps to win a ribbon at the county fair.

Nonetheless, a seed had been planted, and after my father married my mother and discovered that she wished to enroll in college courses, he too enrolled. The classes he signed up for were all art classes.

I Enter the Scene

Mom and Dad were like many, many other young Mormons, both single and married, looking to improve their lots in life through the pursuit of higher education. Brigham Young University was then, as it is today, subsidized by Church tithes and private donations, and thus offered an affordable tuition rate as compared to other universities of equal academic caliber. They found a cozy apartment near the campus to claim as their first joint residence.

Thus it was that I, like the first-born children of many Mormon couples, was born at Provo General Hospital in the winter of 1974. Though I wasn't born exactly nine months after my parents' wedding, I did enter the world before they celebrated their first wedding anniversary. Mom had to miss a few days of class when I was born, but then rushed back to complete her final exams of the semester.

Dad was dutifully taking the art classes for which he had registered, and finding that his love of painting was steadily growing. Unfortunately, he could muster little regard for the academic world and its professors. He felt his teachers were largely a group of frustrated artists who were stuck teaching because they couldn't commit to art.

Dad soon grew tired of hearing his teachers explaining that it simply wasn't possible to make a living and provide for a family as an artist (we'll see that they weren't entirely wrong), and came to resent their encouragement for their students to get real careers, and to engage in art on the side as a hobby. If their students were committed to pursuing art beyond school, they should acquire academic credentials and look for teaching positions. That particular scenario, they insisted, provided the only plausible pathway to make a real living in the art world.

My mom and dad weren't hippies in the traditional picture one might have of hippies. They didn't smoke pot or drive to California in a VW Bus; but Dad's hair was a bit on the long side, he wore facial hair, and there were bell-bottomed jeans in both of my parents' wardrobes.

Not unlike the typical hippie of that era, Dad also developed a deep mistrust of authority figures, along with a desire to chart his own course in life. If someone told him he couldn't do something, that rang like a challenge in his ears. Much credit for my father's artistic career can indeed be attributed to his art professors for telling him to forget about art.

Though I'm a little bit fuzzy about how much longer my parents lasted in school, I do know that before I was old enough to remember, both of my parents dropped out. They moved us back to Idaho, where Dad got a job with an interior designer at a small furniture store. He set up an art studio in half of the little duplex he and Mom purchased, just a few blocks from downtown Burley.

It is here that my memories come into focus, and I can thus begin to tell my story first-hand.

LIGHTWORKS GALLERY

I clearly remember a few things about living in the duplex on Conant Avenue in Burley, Idaho. I remember that there was a large pane of glass and a French door between the kitchen and living room. I remember the way the sunlight would come through the west window in the late afternoon and cast a warm glow into the living room. I remember listening to the William Tell Overture over and over again on Dad's record player.

I remember riding a tricycle and pulling a wagon on the sidewalk in front of the house. I remember playing in the park, just half a block down the street.

I also recollect rolling off the top bunk of the bunk bed I was sharing with my sister Adrienne, and cracking my head open in the middle of the night—an event that necessitated a trip to the emergency room. Hidden in my left brow, I still carry the small scar that resulted from the cut and stitches.

The memories are just flashes—a couple of seconds of imagery from the first three or four years of my life. Fleeting those early memories might be, bearing witness of fairly insignificant events; but during that time, important events did in fact unfold that would set the course for the rest of my life.

It was during this period that Dad proved his interest in art was more than just a passing fancy. At his discretion, he began spending more and more of his time outside of work in his studio, painting. He sought out all of the serious artists he could find in the region, and began to take workshops and classes from them. It wasn't long before Dad began showing and selling his work in local art fairs.

The nearby city of Twin Falls hosted a show in a local park, and with great creativity and an abundance of originality, called the show, "Art in the Park". Mom and Dad loaded Dad's paintings into our car, and drove the entire family to Twin to set up a small booth of Dad's art.

I'm uncertain whether it was in this first show or a subsequent show wherein my parents discovered two important facts. First (and this may have been due to the fact that Dad's work was selling cheap), they discovered that people not only liked my dad's paintings, but they were willing to buy them. Second, they discovered that my mother was a born salesperson.

Mom had been a friend to everyone in high school, easily maneuvering from one group to another, and had graduated as valedictorian. She was great at breaking the ice and starting a conversation, and like her mother, knew how to go the extra mile to please people. She also inherited her father's sales acumen.

While Dad could be pleasant and engaging, he was also soft-spoken, and could sometimes seem a bit awkward and unsure of himself. Mom was the perfect complement and polar opposite: she was enthusiastic and talkative, with an energy that would help encourage interested viewers to move from casual curiosity to passionate purchase.

Mom was endowed with the entrepreneurial spirit of my grandfather, and the bookkeeper's discipline of my grandmother. As soon as they had sold that first artwork, Mom and Dad were convinced that they could build a successful business around the sale of Dad's art. All they needed to turn Dad's passion into the American dream was for Dad to produce a good quantity of art, and the venues wherein Mom could sell it.

It's easy, in retrospect, to call their enthusiasm naiveté; but those first few sales in the park were the spark that ignited their vision of what the future might hold. Those were heady times.

It didn't take Mom and Dad long to realize, however, that local art fairs were never going to provide them the broad exposure they would ultimately need to generate sufficient sales to create a stable living. In order to do that, they would require venues that drew consistent and regular traffic. From my dad's interactions with other artists, he learned that art galleries were the best places to achieve this kind of exposure, and to generate sales.

The problem was that Dad's work wasn't developed enough to get into galleries (or at least this is what my parents thought). They doubted that gallery owners would give a young upstart with little to no experience the time of day, let alone representation.

So my parents did what they would do again and again throughout their lives: they invented. If getting Dad's art into a gallery was unattainable at present, Mom and Dad would simply create their own gallery to show Dad's work. They would provide his representation.

They rented an empty storefront on Oakley Avenue in Burley, just a few blocks from our house, and set about creating the Lightworks Gallery. Dad quit his job at the furniture store, and talked to a few local artists. The next thing we all knew, the gallery was ready for its grand opening.

Opening a gallery in a small town in Southern Idaho should have been the height of folly. As I've already pointed out, the local population was unlikely to be interested in art, and there were no tourists visiting the area. I don't know who my parents thought would be their clients, but Mom and Dad, Mom especially, were masters of making the impossible happen.

As evidence of her resourcefulness, Mom somehow managed to get the governor of Idaho, John Evans, to attend their grand opening, and to cut the ribbon as they opened their doors. The governor happened to be from Burley, but the state capitol in Boise was three hours away. I have no idea how she managed to contact the governor, to coordinate the opening to fit his busy schedule, and to secure his commitment to personally support the event.

I remember seeing a photo of the ribbon cutting ceremony, which made it into the local paper. It's only now, looking back, that this event truly mystifies me. As far as I know, Mom and Dad didn't have any political connections, and I'm certain that the governor could not have attended every business opening in the area. And yet, there he was, smiling as he used a pair of large shears to gleefully cut the ribbon.

Lightworks Gallery was not an instant success. Nonetheless, my parents did a couple of things that helped turn it into a viable business. In addition to selling art, Dad bought all the tools and supplies he would need to run a small framing operation. I suspect that he framed as many family photos for patrons as he did artworks, but the framing helped generate a modest yet steady cash flow.

Dad also taught and hosted art classes in the backroom of the gallery. These classes, along with the framing, helped him connect with the artist community in the area, a community made up of largely casual painters.

Some of the people with whom he connected by means of his framing and teaching, also had enough disposable income to purchase art. A few of those original collectors who met my father and discovered his work would become lifelong friends and loyal collectors.

Of course it didn't hurt that rent in Burley was cheap—very, very cheap. It also bode well that Lightworks Gallery was the closest thing to culture within thirty miles, thereby ensuring that a wine and cheese reception would attract local society, such as it was.

The name of the gallery, Lightworks, was, my dad thought, an inspired choice. Light plays a critical part in painting, and my father aspired to capture the subtleties of light and shadow in his landscape and still-life work.

The problem with the name was that for someone searching through the yellow pages of the phone directory, "Lightworks" suggested something else entirely. Many of the calls, and a good number of the visits to the gallery, were inquiries about chandeliers, track lights, and other lighting fixtures. Though Mom and Dad were good-natured about it, it had to get a bit annoying over time.

OUR FAMILY GROWS

I was born in the winter of 1974, close enough to the end of the year that we could practically call it 1975. My first sister, Adrienne, was born nineteen months later in June of 1976. That's close enough that I can't remember life without my little sister.

I couldn't really pronounce my sister's complicated name, inspired by my dad's mission in France, so I called her "Sissy" for a while, and then, simply "A". Throughout my childhood and teenage years, Adrienne would be my most constant friend. We argued and fought like brothers and sisters do, and I might or might not have encouraged her to sit in an ant pile (a dastardly deed I still hear about to this day). Notwithstanding our differences, a solidarity formed between the two of us, and grew stronger and more sure as our family developed (and especially as Mom and Dad led us on wild and sometimes dark adventures).

In 1978, my second sister, Yvette, was born, but her birth was complicated by the fact that she was born a month premature, and spent the first two weeks of her life in the hospital. I was far too young to know what was going on, yet have since been told that the way the doctors treated my mother and new baby sister didn't sit well with my parents. The doctors had insisted on plugging my mom into a heart monitor during the delivery, and had poked and prodded my sister after her birth, causing a great deal of wailing and crying. Mom and Dad felt this was all unnecessary, and didn't care for the doctors' attitudes of superiority. The seeds of mistrust of the medical establishment and modern medicine were planted, seeds that would soon sprout into a full-scale rejection.

Though not old enough to sense this tension, I was old enough at three-and-a-half to appreciate the momentous occasion when Yvette was finally brought home. I loved holding my little sister, and when she was asleep in her crib, I would drag my blanket off my bed and crawl under her crib, so that I could sleep close to the wondrous little creature slumbering right above me. I took many naps this way, and there were mornings when my mother would find me asleep under the crib, having somehow managed to find my way there in the dark of the night.

Shalece, sister number three, was born in July of 1979, two weeks shy of Yvette's first birthday. I've spent my entire post-pubescent life striving not to think too hard about that timing, and I would encourage you, dear reader, to pass quickly by that date so you too can avoid uncomfortable pondering.

Shalece was curly-haired and doll-like. At four-and-a-half, I was still young enough to appreciate having a new baby in the house (though Yvette was also still very much a baby), but I was old enough to be deeply disappointed that Shalece had the gaul to be born a girl, rather than a boy. In the five-and-a-half years since my parents had married, they had created a family with four children—by modern standards, a large family—and it seemed a bit unfair to have given

20

Adrienne two baby sisters, yet not to have bothered giving me a brother. Little did I know that my parents were only halfway finished having children, and that eventually, the boys would actually outnumber the girls.

In the meantime, I learned to make do with my sisters. I had to admit that Shalece, with her doll-like curly locks, was adorable. The four of us would come to form a tight bond that would endure throughout our lives.

BUCKMINSTER FULLER

As our family grew, and as Lightworks Gallery began to experience a modest level of success, Dad discovered the writings of Buckminster Fuller. Fuller was an inventor (though he preferred to think of himself as a discoverer), a visionary theorist, and an architect of sorts. He aligned his thinking with the post-World War II zeitgeist of utopian thinking. Much like Frank Lloyd Wright, a generation before him, or Paolo Soleri a generation after, Fuller believed society and humankind could be fundamentally changed for the better through thoughtful architecture and reasoned city planning.

Fuller was particularly interested in creating practical and inexpensive shelter and transportation. If the world could finally shelter and provide for its inhabitants a comfortable living, there would be no more need to wage wars over scarce resources. Fuller coined the term "Dymaxion" to summarize what he was striving to achieve: maximum gain of advantage from minimal energy input.

It would have been easy for the world to write Fuller off as an impractical visionary and affable weirdo had it not been for his success in advocating for the geodesic dome. Though

Fuller didn't invent the geodesic dome, he did innovate on the idea, and managed to obtain the U.S. patent for its design. His advocacy of the geometric structure brought it to prominence in the 1950s and '60s.

I'm dramatically oversimplifying Fuller's contributions and philosophy, but what's important to my story is the fact that his idealism was highly contagious to those with starry-eyed tendencies: people like my dad.

Dad read one of Fuller's books and his imagination was ignited. My dad saw the geodesic dome as the future, and he wanted to be a part of it. As soon as he learned the fundamentals of the dome, he decided that he was going to build one, and that our family was going to live in it.

I remember Dad explaining countless times over the years to curious neighbors how the dome design provided the maximum internal volume with the least exterior surface area. This was all somewhat abstract for a kid to understand; I knew only that people were invariably dubious about the project.

Dad was able to convince my mom, however, and that was all that mattered. They sold the duplex on Oakley Avenue, and purchased three quarters of an acre of land five miles west of Burley, amidst farmland and sparsely populated countryside. They also purchased a single-wide mobile home, which they parked on the property for us to live in while Dad built the dome.

The plan was simple. Dad would hire someone to dig out the foundation, he would purchase the simple materials needed to construct the dome, and would work evenings and weekends to complete the structure. He and my mom decided they would pay cash for everything, so that when the home was completed there would be no mortgage.

Mom and Dad expected that if things went well, the dome would be done in six to eight months. With a spring date to

23

launch the project, the dome should be ready for our occupation before the winter was upon us.

Though Dad was neither an architect nor a builder, his ambitions were not completely quixotic. After all, Grandpa Horejs had built two homes during my father's youth, and Dad had helped him with both. Dad learned how to use all the tools in Grandpa's extensive woodshop, and he knew that he would be able to contract for the work that he was unable to do himself. He could also turn directly to my grandfather whenever he needed advice, although Grandpa was among those who were deeply sceptical about the project.

Ultimately, Grandpa, a trained surveyor, swallowed his doubts and helped survey the site before the foundation was dug. In addition, he provided input on various aspects of the project, including the carpentry, the plumbing, and the electrical. His assistance was always welcomed and appreciated.

I'm not aware of there being any official blueprints for the building of the dome. However, I do remember visiting an architect in Twin Falls who had built his home in lava caves, and I assume that this architect offered his expertise regarding fundamental engineering issues involved with constructing the dome.

Luckily for Dad, he was building on land governed by the county; thus, there were no zoning or inspection requirements. One could build whatever one wanted in the county, and no one would stop the construction to ask questions. This was good, because as the project progressed, the design, plans, and materials continually evolved. Dad was building a vision, and visions don't always fit neatly into tidy blueprints.

As I plumb the deep recesses of my memory, I manage to retrieve the sights and sounds of a backhoe moving earth from within a fifty foot diameter circle that would serve as the dome's foundation. I also recall a cement truck pouring the concrete for the footings, and the sight of rebar sticking out of the circular foundation. Dad explained that the rebar would tie the superstructure of the dome to the foundation. The foundation for the dome was quite different from a traditional slab foundation. Most homes have a solid foundation that serves as the footprint for the home. The dome's foundation was an eighteen inch wide ring that ran along the outer circumference of the planned structure. The outer shell of the dome would rest on this foundation. After the outer layer of the dome was finished, a second circular foundation would be poured in the center of the dome. A masonry tower would be configured to rise in the middle of the dome. The floors of the dome were designed to radiate outward from this tower, and to be supported by cinder block columns erected at strategic points.

Though we would live on four or five different levels, only the first floor would cover the entire area of the dome. The upper levels were to be comprised of triangles and half circles that would radiate from the tower in a circular pattern.

While there were a couple of other dome homes in the area, Dad's design was the most enterprising and ambitious. The other domes were built like typical houses stuck inside of a bubble. Dad was throwing away centuries of interior architecture to build something entirely new.

Single-Wide

The manufactured home, or trailer home, doesn't receive a lot of respect in American culture. The idea that Henry Ford's assembly line should be employed to construct homes in a factory has never taken root with the country's gentry, and mobile-home dwellers are generally viewed to be from a lower socio-economic class.

In this regard, Burley was a trailer house magnet. A scarcity of good-paying jobs, and a need for migrant farm workers, led to a boom in manufactured home sales. There were a variety of trailer parks inside and outside the city limits, and the countryside was scattered with trailers on random lots.

Some of those who lived in trailers on a more permanent basis tried diligently to spruce up their appearance by adding decks or by landscaping their lots. There is really only so much one can do, however, for a house that is basically made out of tin, and necessarily designed with axles that can be no wider than what will fit on a single lane of America's highways.

Idaho's harsh winters and windy weather weren't kind to the trailer homes either. No mobile home could long withstand the ravages perpetrated by this environment before beginning to look somewhat bedraggled.

Fairly or not, there was a perception among Burley's population that mobile homes were mostly populated with "white trash" (to coin the term popular in the local vernacular) or with hispanics. No self-respecting family would stoop to live in a trailer if there were any other alternative.

My parents believed our situation was a little different. We weren't making a permanent residence in a trailer: we were merely planning to live in one for a few months while Dad built the dome. It would therefore be more like camping than residing.

The trailer, which my parents bought for a few thousand dollars, was white with green trim. That green exterior trim was harmonious with the interior's harvest gold vinyl flooring and appliances, and almost perfectly matched by the shaggy green carpet in the living room.

The small kitchen was situated at one end of the house, complete with a gas stove, a small refrigerator, and a built-in table with a bench seat and a couple of chairs. The cupboards were finished with a dark fake-wood veneer.

A small hallway led from the living room, first to a small bedroom, then to the bathroom/laundry room, and finally to the "master bedroom". The master bedroom was a scant few square feet larger than the first bedroom, with a slightly larger closet, but was otherwise just another room in which to sleep.

I wasn't yet five when we moved into the trailer, and I don't remember it feeling small or cramped. I'm sure I just thought of living in it as another great adventure. We were moving out of town into the open countryside, and Dad was going to build us a great big bubble house. It all sounded like so much fun!

Because we were in the county, there were no water, sewer, or trash services. Mom and Dad hired the digging of a well and septic tank, and the trash was burned in a pit at one corner of our lot. A large white propane tank behind the trailer provided fuel for heating and cooking in the trailer.

Our property sat about half a mile past the five-mile-corner on State Highway 30. This highway had been the main thoroughfare between all of the major towns that had sprung up along the Snake River. It had carried traffic and commerce between Burley and Twin Falls to the west, and Pocatello to the east.

Small towns and burgs had sprung up along the highway around gas stations and convenience stores that serviced the automobile traffic running on the thoroughfare.

Much of the traffic had died away when the federal government commissioned Interstate 84, which ran on the north side of the Snake River. Highway 30 ran east to west on the south side of the river. The drop in traffic brought with it a drop in the fortunes of those who lived along the old highway. In fact, locals actually began calling it "The Old Highway", and though the state maintained the double laned road and plowed it during the winter, it was primarily used by local traffic. Farmers from the area drove into, and out of town on the highway, and during the harvest season, large trucks filled with potatoes, corn, or grain, would make their way to the potato cellars and grain elevators in Burley.

The highway sat up on a bank along the southeast edge of our property. Our trailer sat parallel to the highway, and because the walls were pretty thin, we could hear cars and trucks roaring by all day, and with only a little less frequency, all night as well. The amount of traffic on the Old Highway was probably only a fraction of what was moving on the freeway, but it was enough that, to this day, I am nearly immune to the noise of traffic.

My sister Adrienne and I found the move to be a lark. Looking back, I know that our lot in the country wasn't very large, and that it was devoid of trees; but for small children like us, it was a world within itself.

The triangular plot had three distinct geographic areas. At the front of the property, along the graveled road that broke off from the highway and from which our driveway ran, was a small drainage ditch. This ditch was empty much of the time; however, every few days during the late spring and summer, due to some irrigation schedule which was a complete mystery to us, the ditch would fill and run like a small creek.

Even though Dad had installed a steel pipe under our driveway, some days there was so much water that the pipe couldn't handle it all. The happy result of this situation was the formation of a small lake (or large puddle) of excess water enveloping the driveway.

The status of that ditch was the first thing my sister and I would check when we awoke every morning. We were delighted to find water in the driveway, because that meant the course of our day was set. We would eat breakfast, quickly dress in shorts or swimming suits, and then head down the short driveway to gleefully splash around in our own private lake.

With some strategic damming along the driveway, we could turn the puddled water on the uphill side into a lake that would reach halfway or more up a five-year-old's shins. We would spend hours wading around in the ditch, playing games, racing stick boats, and throwing in rocks to see who could create the biggest splash. The water was cold, and the Idaho morning air was chilly, but we didn't care: we were enthralled in our childhood heaven!

On days when the ditch wasn't running, we could explore the weeds and sagebrush that covered most of the rest of the property. The sage was home to jackrabbits and meadowlarks, and we enjoyed scaring up both.

In the farthest corner of the property, a clump of willows grew out of a marshy area that was steadily watered from an irrigation drainage pipe that ran under the highway. Although it never received enough water to turn into another ditch, the ground was consistently damp, sometimes even soggy like a wet sponge. The willows had sufficient water to thrive. They grew tall enough to dwarf our diminutive heights, and thick enough to create a jungle-like foliage. We would wander into the thicket and pretend to be explorers lost in the wilds of central Africa.

It should be noted that up to this point in my life, my family did not own a television set. It wasn't that we couldn't have afforded one. I'm sure Mom and Dad could have bought one if they wanted. However, because they were already beginning to brace themselves against the conventions of society, the tyranny of the television seemed to them a logical bond to break.

This didn't mean that my sisters and I were deprived of entertainment. Mom was an avid reader, and some of my earliest memories are of her reading stories to us, and then progressing to longer books. These books opened a world of imagination, and our childish pretendings would often be based on the characters and settings we discovered in the literature she read to us.

I learned to read long before I ever set foot in a school. Our family was consistently among the most frequent visitors to the small public library that was conveniently located a short block away from Lightworks Gallery.

This didn't mean I was happy with our lack of TV. Quite the contrary.

My maternal grandparents had several television sets in their home. When we visited, I was introduced to the world of late '70s and early '80s television. I especially loved watching CHiPs, M*A*S*H (apparently I had an affinity for programing built around acronyms) and later, Knight Rider. Unfortunately, Grandma and Grandpa Summers lived three hours away in Layton, Utah, so our visits to them and their televisions were less frequent than I would have wished.

Being deprived of so basic a human right as television naturally meant that I placed a high premium on it. When visiting friends' homes, I would try to convince them that playing was a bore, and that what we really should do was watch some TV (even though the only thing on might have been a soap opera or the evening news). I would go to great lengths to time my visits so that I could watch reruns of Star Trek—I loved Spock and Captain Kirk.

I can see now that our life without television was actually pretty amazing. A life without the lazy entertainment of the tube encouraged me and my siblings to employ our imaginations and to devise our own adventures. These adventures only increased as we settled in to life in the country, and for a time, we were too distracted to worry about not having a TV.

Hence we settled into the trailer house in the spring of 1979. Dad began purchasing supplies, and we watched with interest and anticipation as he began building the dome.

Construction Begins

The first supplies to arrive were rebar, styrofoam and chicken wire, the key components to the first phase of the dome. The steel rebar came in long bars, tied together with wire. The foam came in large, rectangular sheets, eight inches thick. The chicken wire came in a six-foot-high roll.

I can only imagine what neighbors thought as they drove by. This was a home construction site unlike anything they would have seen before.

Dad began his work by carefully measuring and cutting the styrofoam into triangles. These weren't normal triangles, however. The triangles would have to be fitted together at angles as the structure of the dome rose. This meant that each triangle had to be cut at a perfect angle to fit with the triangles next to it, and those above and below. The triangles would be put together to form hexagons, which would then all join together in an arching curve to create the dome.

Dad loved to quote Buckminster Fuller about how inherently strong this structure was, and to tout the natural integrity of the design. The construction process was beautifully simple. The foam panels were tied together with wire and rebar, and the only tools needed were a metal saw to cut the rebar and a handsaw to cut the foam. On the first day of construction, the first couple of foam panels were secured to the foundation, and the structure of the dome began to rise from the Idaho countryside. Each day more panels were cut and tied together, and progress was steady . . .

Except all of this work took longer than planned.

It turned out it was harder than expected to align the panels at the perfect angles, and tying them together was a challenge. The first days turned into weeks, and then those weeks melted into the months of the summer.

Dad, who was still running the gallery, couldn't work on the dome every day. There were several days taken off in July when my sister, Shalece, was born. It soon became clear that the plans to complete construction over the summer and into the fall had been overly ambitious. By late August, the construction of the dome's shell had progressed only to the second story.

Oblivious to the slow progress of the dome, Adrienne and I had a wonderful time that first summer. We were allowed to roam our property and the construction site at will. Apparently, the large panels of foam didn't pose enough danger to cause worry about our presence on the site.

The sun rose early on those summer mornings, and thanks to daylight savings time, it stayed light until almost ten o'clock at night. Our adventures might begin at the ditch in the morning, and then progress through the different geographies of the property throughout the day, with a break for lunch, and later for popsicles.

We began to make friends with kids in the neighborhood and from our church congregation. Since we had no television, we wove our playtime narratives purely from our own imaginations. When we could, we went to our friends' houses to watch TV.

I remember those days of the first summer as a magical time, carefree and filled with the constant promise and allure of adventure. We were allowed to wander down the country road to play with friends, or they were free to come and join the fun at our place.

The Idaho summer was hot and dry. Temperatures would cool down into the fifties most nights, but the daytime temperatures could rise into the nineties; a temperature of one hundred degrees was not unusual.

Some days Mom would take us to the municipal pool, or to a park in town. Mom and Dad's business at the gallery was growing, and Dad was continuing to paint while he ran the business and constructed the dome.

Even though headway on the dome was slow, our lives were full of promise. Summer wound down, and soon slipped into fall. Fall brought the harvest for our neighbors, and cooler temperatures for all of us.

Halloween came and went, and winter crept stealthily into the countryside.

THE GODDAMN WIND BLOWS

Winters are cold in Idaho. It can snow enough for several feet of accumulated depth in the valleys, and up to seven or eight feet in the surrounding mountains. This is ample snow for skiing, and there is in fact a minor ski resort in the mountains twenty-five miles or so southeast of Burley. The ski season isn't long; however, there is enough snow to have decent skiing from late November into February.

It is cold and grey through much of the winter. That being said, neither the cold, nor the overcast sky, is the defining feature of the Southern Idaho winter. That would be the wind.

The Snake River Valley is wide and flat, and runs parallel to the jetstream. When a low-pressure system pushes down from Alaska and Canada and moves across the region, there is nothing to stop the wind that follows it. The breeze can start in the plains of Eastern Oregon, and by the time it makes its way to Burley, it is likely to be a full-on gale.

They call Chicago the "Windy City", but I submit that theirs is just a breeze when compared to the Idaho wind. The Idaho wind can blow strongly and steadily for months on end during the winter, occasionally reaching hurricane speeds.

I don't remember many notable days that first winter—one cold day blends into the next in those distant memories. I do, however, remember one particularly blustery Sunday morning.

Dad had taken Adrienne and me to church as the wind howled on that Sunday morning. Mom must have stayed home with Yvette and Shalece, because coming home from church it was just my dad, Adrienne, and me in Dad's sky-blue Lincoln Continental. As we came around the five-mile corner and neared our home, we could see that something was wrong up ahead.

The sky was mostly clear, but it appeared that snow was blowing across the highway from our property. As we drew closer, the small white detritus drifting across the road was suddenly joined by several large, oddly shaped white blocks. Everything was moving across the highway and then beyond, covering the landscape to the east.

"Shit!" I heard Dad growl as he pulled the Lincoln off the highway, down the short gravel road, and into our driveway.

My sister and I, who had both been sitting in the backseat (most likely without seatbelts), jumped to our feet on the floorboard, grabbed the back of the front seat, and through eyes wide with wonder, gazed at the spectacle ahead.

I knew that cursing was bad—really, really bad, according to my mother—but I'm not sure if Adrienne, only three or four at the time, knew the significance of the word that was still hanging in the air. We both understood from the tone of Dad's voice, and from the heavy electricity pulsing through the silence of the car as we stood staring at the building site, that Dad was angry—very angry.

The dome at this point was comprised of a full ring of styrofoam and metal, and rose almost two stories from the foundation; a kind of bizarre Stonehenge. Or at least it *had* been a full ring when we left for church services earlier that morning.

Now the entire west side of the structure had collapsed and folded in on itself. Large chunks of foam were missing, leaving gaping holes. Even as we watched in fascinated horror, another large triangle of foam was wrenched free by the fierce wind and blown past the windshield of the Lincoln, tumbled up the embankment, and whisked across the highway.

A heavy silence hung in the idling Lincoln as Adrienne and I followed the trajectory of yet another triangle, unable to avert our gaze. For a time, Dad seemed dazed, frozen in place—unable to fathom the scene unfolding before him.

Then suddenly the car's engine thundered to life, and the Lincoln leaped forward, hurtling toward the stacks of unshaped foam where they lay staked down in front of our mobile home. As the grill of the Lincoln made contact with the foam, Adrienne and I were thrown against the back of the front bench-seat.

Adrienne screamed, and I felt terrified tears stinging my cheeks. Styrofoam exploded in every direction before being grabbed by the wind to join the foam already careening away from the dome.

Dad must have applied the brakes before we hit, otherwise the heavy car would have plowed right through the foam and crashed into the side of our trailer house. There was no indication of uncertainty, hesitation, or remorse on Dad's part with regard to his behavior. After the car shuddered to a halt, Dad threw the column-mounted gearshift into reverse, backed across the yard, braked, and then surged forward to ram the foam again.

As we made impact a second time, I saw through my tears the back door of the mobile home fly open, and my nightgown clad mother, mouth wide open in a desperate shout. We couldn't hear her over the roar of the car and the screaming of the wind, but I could read her lips as she repeatedly howled my father's name in desperation.

"John! John! John! John . . ."

As with most mobile homes, ours was elevated on its axles and placed on blocks, so the front and back doors, both of which were on the side of the house facing the driveway, sat up three or four feet from the ground. We had a set of wood steps at the front door, but there were none at the back door, which meant that my mom would have had to leap to get down to the ground. Instead, she disappeared for a moment as she hustled to the front door.

While Mom hustled to exit the trailer, Dad backed up for another run at the foam. He forcefully hit the foam head-on, just as my mother reached the side of the car, whereupon she started banging on the passenger window, even as she yanked the car door open. Luckily, Dad decided to discontinue his demolition derby, and the Lincoln sat still as Mom hurriedly pulled first my sister, and then me, from the back seat of the car.

As we were enveloped in the biting wind and swirling foam beads, I heard Dad mutter, "Goddamn wind."

"John! John!" My mother screamed. "Stop!"

This finally seemed to get Dad's attention. He looked up at her, and his eyes slowly came into focus.

"You could have hurt the children!" Mom cried. "You could have hurt yourself, and wrecked the car!"

Dad didn't respond, but turned the engine off and slowly got out of the car. Mom hustled my sister and me into the trailer, pulled a coat on over her nightgown, slipped her feet into a pair of boots, and headed back outside to join my father in the tempest.

Adrienne and I, having ceased our crying, and being somewhat shell-shocked, stood peering out the living room window. Mom and Dad began gathering foam from the front yard and the loose panels from the now mangled dome, and piling them back into the stacks next to the trailer. Soon they had everything they could get from the site and yard, and began roaming out over the fields downwind of our property. This foam rescue mission took several hours that Sunday afternoon, and continued on Monday, after the wind had finally died down. Large panels and broken pieces were retrieved from distances spanning two miles.

Though there could have been other sources of foam in the county, friends and neighbors would later claim that they saw chunks of the dome as far away as Declo, some twenty miles from our property in Burley.

Reconstructing the damaged dome that first winter was frustrating, I'm sure, for my Dad, and was a major setback in progressing toward the completion of the enterprise. Unfortunately, this was far from the last setback. There was much more cursing and frustration, not to mention wind, ahead.

A PROFESSIONAL ARTIST

Part of the challenge for my parents as they worked to construct the dome was that they were also trying to build my father's career as a professional fine artist, and to maximize the success of the gallery. Because they had decided to build the dome without incurring any debt, it was essential that they generate art sales so that they could keep food on the table and purchase construction materials.

Mom and Dad were working long days at the gallery, but they were also beginning to venture throughout the West, looking for galleries that would agree to represent my father and market his work. Because they had been effective in selling Dad's work in the Lightworks Gallery and at art shows, they now felt more confident about approaching galleries—Dad had proven himself to be a bonafide seller.

Their first success came when Tuesday's Child, a small gallery in Boise, agreed to show Dad's work. Though the gallery would soon go out of business, they managed to sell some of Dad's pieces, and moreover, opened the door for Dad to work with an established art consultant, as well as with other galleries in Idaho's capital and largest city. Mom and Dad had now launched a new phase in Dad's art career.

Slowly, Dad began shifting more and more of his time to painting, which shift presented its own set of problems. In order to stock his own gallery, provide inventory for the Boise galleries, and prepare for outdoor shows, Dad had to spend more time at the easel. As he was also determined to continue building the dome, something had to give: there are only so many hours in a day.

Dad had been maintaining a fairly consistent teaching schedule, giving workshops, and offering classes to mostly older women who lived in Burley and the surrounding communities. He elected to reduce his teaching in order to paint more, which meant that we lost some revenue and the financial stability that had come through his regular teaching.

Dad also brought his brother Doug into the gallery part-time to help with the framing business. While this helped Dad spend more time painting, Doug's wages further reduced our family's cash flow.

A chaotic cycle was set in motion. A sale would occur, either at the Lightworks Gallery, through a show, or perhaps in Boise. Early on, Dad's art had been selling for several hundred dollars per piece, but was at this time selling for several thousand dollars. Money would flow in from a sale, enabling Mom to stock up on groceries and other necessities, and allowing Dad to purchase building materials.

Dad would then spend some time working on the dome, and continue working until the money began to run out, which would usually be within a few weeks. This would lead Dad back to the studio and the gallery to generate more art and to wait for further sales.

Mom was helping in the gallery too, and did everything she could to support Dad's efforts. It was challenging, however, for her to undertake sales efforts at the same time she was rearing four young children, two of them babies, Adrienne a toddler, and me not yet in school.

41

I have a hard time imagining how Mom and Dad juggled it all. I remember during this period that my sisters and I spent a lot of time at the gallery. My "almost twin" sisters, Yvette and Shalece, played and slept in a pen behind the gallery's checkout counter. Adrienne and I played in the back room, in the cellar under the building, and (a thought horrifying to today's parents) unattended in either the parking lot or in the alley behind the gallery. We roamed the neighborhood around the gallery, and somehow managed to avoid being run over or kidnapped.

All this juggling among building, painting, and retailing meant that not one of the three undertakings developed as quickly as my parents might have hoped. Instead, there was at best slow and sporadic progress in each endeavor.

I Come Dangerously Close
to Beginning Kindergarten

In August of 1980, Mom and her friend, Deanne Bell, who lived just down the street from us in a little white clapboard house, loaded me and Deanne's son, Todd, into the Bell's station wagon, and drove us out to the county kindergarten in Springdale.

Burley had two grade schools, a middle school for fifth and sixth graders, a junior high, and a high school. These schools served families from a broad geographic area that included the entire town of Burley, together with hundreds of square miles in the surrounding Cassia County.

For some reason, however, the kindergarten was located in the small farming village of Springdale, six miles east of Burley. Before the schools in Burley had begun drawing the farm children from the neighboring communities, the building had served as a school for the area children of all grades. Now the building was a dedicated kindergarten, and each year the school administrators held an open house to register local children, and to introduce them to their teachers.

43

I was nervous about the prospect of beginning school, though probably no more so than the typical child. Memories have faded concerning the details of the kindergarten orientation. However, I likely expressed some of the same misgivings about attending school as have been expressed by five-year-olds since time immemorial.

It is a testament to my mother's enormous love for me, and perhaps indicative of her over-protective nature, that she heeded my protestations, and began looking for an alternative to the school in Springdale. One can be sure there were few choices in small-town Burley, yet by fortunate happenstance, or divine intervention, a brave educator was just then opening a private Montessori school not two blocks from Lightworks Gallery.

Notwithstanding the issue of there being my tuition to consider, Mom and Dad registered me for the fall kindergarten class, and thus launched my education outside of the public school system. Because they signed Adrienne up for the Montessori pre-school, Mom's child-care load declined by half that September.

My Montessori experience was idyllic. Instead of being stuck in a classroom with a bunch of other five-year-old students, Montessori took more of a one-room schoolhouse approach. Students across all the grades, from kindergarten through sixth, were together in a large room, from which they would break to undertake various activities.

That first year, the school was held in what had formerly been a Mormon church building. Lecture was given in the chapel. Individual subjects were taught in the Sunday school classrooms. The pre-school was conducted downstairs in the basement.

Thanks to Mom's tutoring, I came into the school already knowing how to read. My reading and innate curiosity provided me an advantage in picking up other basic scholastic skills, and allowed me to quickly proceed through the Montessori lessons.

I particularly remember that math was taught using tiny yellow blocks. The block set consisted of small one-by-one blocks, long ten-by-one chains, square ten-by-ten blocks, and large ten-by-ten-by-ten cubes. Manipulating those blocks by adding them together, subtracting from them, and multiplying was, I now realize, a wonderful way for a five-year-old to learn the basic concepts of arithmetic. Numbers became a very concrete concept, and I advanced rapidly through the assignments. By the time I reached the second grade level, I had a facility with long division, a concept my friends who went to public school wouldn't begin to tackle until the end of the third grade.

The Montessori approach also put lesson planning squarely in the students' hands. We weren't assigned specific lessons to complete each day; rather, at the beginning of the week, we were given a "contract sheet". This sheet was a grid of boxes that had the days of the week along the top, and the subjects along the left side. We would each examine the required lesson material for the coursework, and then assign ourselves lessons for the coming week. We could tackle the lessons in any way we desired, thereby setting our own schedule for our education.

Some students might complete assignments in a linear manner, a lesson in each subject every day. Others would tackle all the lessons in a particular subject on a specific day of the week, for instance doing all of their math lessons on Monday, all of their social studies on Tuesday, their reading assignments on Wednesday, and so on. The instructors would let students do whatever they wanted, as long as they completed the "contract" and progressed through the lessons.

I soon figured out that with a little concentration and discipline, I could complete the entire week's tasks by midday on Tuesday, which would leave me the rest of the week to do whatever I wished. Once finished with all of my schoolwork, I would usually fill the rest of the week with art projects, pleasure reading, or playing in the churchyard.

If I became bored, I frequently set up a contract for the following week, and completed it ahead of schedule. Before long, I had a five or six weeks' surplus of completed assignments. By the second grade, I felt like I owned that school. I was learning about the world and acquiring a host of scholastic skills. More importantly, I was learning to be self-motivated and self-directed.

I may not have owned the local public library, but I was a major stockholder: at the very least, I was one of its best clients.

As noted previously, the library was located just a block away from Mom and Dad's gallery. Lucky for me, it was about the same distance from the Montessori school. Before I ever started school, Mom would check out stacks of children's books for me, and I would read them over and over before our next visit to the library.

Once I was in school, I was allowed to get my own library card. I remember the small pink card that had my name typed on it, together with a small metal plate upon which my patron identification number was engraved. The librarians embossed my ID number onto the check-out sheet at the front of each borrowed book. I treasured that library card, and protected it in the small manilla envelope in which the librarian placed it before putting it in my outreached hand.

During each visit to the library, I checked out eight books, the limit for a patron to have on his card. I voraciously read through the stack of books at home, returned to the library as soon as I could, and traded in the trove for eight more. In this manner, I read every Hardy Boy, Nancy Drew, Little House on the Prairie, Narnia, and Great Brain book in the library, along with every other children's and young adult book the library offered from its modest collection.

Unfortunately, it happened that Burley couldn't long sustain a private Montessori school. There weren't enough students with the means to pay tuition; the school struggled to pay its rent and teachers' salaries. The enterprise hobbled along for a couple of years before the founder finally moved on to other pursuits, leaving the parents to take over the monumental task of keeping the school going.

To save on rent, the parents moved the school from the church building into a brick house on Overland Avenue that had been converted for commercial use. Though several of the original teachers remained on staff to instruct the diminishing student body, it was soon abundantly clear that the school could not survive. Halfway through my fourth year in attendance, the doors were permanently closed, and my private school days were ended.

Despite their continued misgivings about the public school system, Mom and Dad had no choice but to enroll Adrienne and me in the local elementary school district. Adrienne was placed in the second grade, while I entered the school as a third grader, and was assigned to Mr. Gerard's class.

I experienced an adjustment going to a classroom filled with students my own age, and studying in a considerably more regimented fashion than I had studied at the Montessori school. In some ways, however, I felt a bit like Superman who, coming to Earth from Krypton, realizes that he has a special set of abilities that the difference in environment has provided him.

My new public school peers were still learning basic multiplication, something I could breeze through. Many were also struggling to read at a third grade level. When we were tested, I was assessed to be reading at a seventh grade level. I continued to push myself forward, reading ahead in the textbooks and completing homework days in advance of due dates.

I soon learned, though, that it was a bad idea to show off my academic skills, or to let fellow students know that school was easy for me. Their nasty glances told me that they thought I was both a nerd and a kiss-up to the teacher. I couldn't understand why I was looked down upon by my peers for doing a good job on the work we were all assigned.

My utter disinterest with, and complete ineptitude at sports further lowered my status among my fellow students. I did my best to blend in and make friends with the other geeks.

A Revised Construction Schedule

By the summer of 1980, it was clear that we had overshot the scheduled six months designated for the construction of the dome. It was also obvious that our family was destined to spend a second winter in the mobile home. Construction was progressing, but ever so slowly. The structure was taking on a dome shape now. It was requiring substantial time to tie all of the foam together, and proving difficult and cumbersome to frame the windows, all of which were triangular in shape, necessitating complex geometric cuts.

Even though Dad and Mom were still optimistic that it wouldn't take long once the shell was constructed, we had now fully settled into life in the mobile home. What had once been deemed an adventure in a temporary domicile had become our long term reality. And while life in a trailer was far from glamorous, it was our norm. Meals were cooked, chores were done, stories were read, and the Horejs family saga slowly unfolded.

Summer turned to fall, and as we knew it would, fall became winter. Construction slowed as the unremitting winter storms blew through. The bitterly cold days often made it impossible for Dad to build.

As children, my sisters and I were unbothered by the frustrations my parents endured. We had shelter, and didn't care at this point that it was in a mobile home. We had food, and we had a father and mother who loved us and loved each other. We felt secure.

More importantly, we thought it was awesome that the foundation of the dome filled with moisture over the course of the winter. The foundation trapped melting snow and rain, and soon the water was several feet deep. This made working on the dome much more difficult, but my sisters and I, along with neighborhood friends, discovered that we had our own kid-sized lake!

The scraps of Dad's foam panels were capable of bearing the weight of small children. Dad didn't protest when we used scrap pieces of foam as rafts, and propelled them around the lake with sticks and poles. The lake nearly covered the entirety of the foundation, which as I mentioned earlier, was nearly fifty feet in diameter: plenty of room to stage pirate battles.

The rafts weren't particularly stable, and we inevitably ended up with soaked feet and worse when we capsized. We didn't care. This was living!

Construction picked up again in the summer of '81, but then slackened in the winter, only to revive again in the summers of '82, then '83, and '84. By then the outer structure of the dome was fully formed into an honest-to-goodness geodesic dome.

Dad hired a concrete company to spray the inside of the structure with gunite, a watered-down cement that was shot through a pressurized hose. (The main application for gunite was the inside of tunnels, which wasn't much different from the effect that was created once the dark grey concrete was in place on the interior walls of the dome.) Dad then covered the window and door openings with multiple layers of plastic to help keep moisture out.

It must have been incredibly frustrating to see how slowly the project advanced. Though there was steady progress, the completion of the dome seemed to loom further and further into the distant future. While much had been done, there was no real end in sight.

Uncle Doug Ruins a Surprise

"Are you hoping for a boy or girl?" my uncle Doug asked.

Adrienne and I were silent for a moment, confused. I was nine at the time, and as I've alluded, at least as smart as any other nine-year-old. I couldn't, however, comprehend what Doug was asking.

Doug, who looked very much like my father, was younger than Dad by a couple of years, and was even more soft-spoken. Doug and his wife, Cindy, had five kids, our cousins, who were all about the same ages as me and my sisters. We were friendly with our cousins, and whenever we got together, happy chaos reigned.

Though I spent a lot of time with his children, I don't remember having spent much time conversing directly with Uncle Doug, which was another reason this conversation was so disorienting.

"I don't know," I finally shrugged, "a boy, I guess?"

"What's that?" my mom asked from across the room, overhearing the gist of the conversation.

"I was just asking if they were hoping for a boy or a girl," Doug replied.

"Oh!!!" Mom exclaimed. "Come on kids, run out and play!"

"THEY DON'T KNOW!" Mom mouthed to Uncle Doug.

"Oops, sorry," Doug replied, his face blushing.

That night, Mom and Dad sat us down in the living room of the trailer.

"We have something we want to tell you," Mom said. "We want to tell you before someone else does."

My sisters and I looked on expectantly.

"We were going to surprise you, but I guess this is surprise enough," Mom continued. "We're going to have a baby!"

It took a moment for this to sink in.

"When?" I asked.

"Hooray!" Adrienne shouted.

"Yippee!" Yvette, now six, exclaimed.

Shalece, five, started crying, but that was normal—we thought of her as a bit of a crybaby at this point. She had been the baby of the family for longer than any of the rest of us, so perhaps this was to be expected.

"Will it be a boy or a girl?" Adrienne asked.

"Yes," Dad said.

"Which?" I persisted.

"A boy or a girl," Dad replied.

Exasperated, we turned to Mom.

"We don't know," she said. "At least that can be a surprise."

Looking back, I'm a bit dumbfounded, and find it hard to fathom what Mom and Dad were thinking. Did they imagine Mom would make it all the way to delivery without telling us she was expecting? Were we naive enough that we wouldn't have noticed her ever expanding belly? It seems unlikely, especially considering how big her fifth child would ultimately be. On the other hand, she was then some six or seven months along and we hadn't yet noticed, so maybe Mom and Dad's subterfuge hadn't been so far-fetched.

My parents' desire to hide the pregnancy was far from the most shocking aspect of the pregnancy and impending delivery. That would be revealed when we met Janet Bingham, Mom's midwife.

Home delivery wasn't exactly rare in Southern Idaho during the 1970s and '80s—Janet had a robust business—but my parents' circumstances made a home delivery seem less than ideal. Our mobile home was not commodious. We were six miles away from the hospital. What if something were to go wrong?

On the other hand, a home delivery would cost less than a hospital birth, and this was one more opportunity to refute the establishment. I was old enough to know that there was something unusual about the idea of my mom having her baby at home, yet not sufficiently mature to articulate any misgivings. I was learning to shrug and accept Mom and Dad's plans without asking too many questions. If I had asked, they would likely have expounded the advantages of a natural birth at home, in contrast to the disadvantages of a drug-induced, monitor-dependent birth in the hospital. I had already heard that speech given to friends and extended family, and the last thing I wanted was to hear it again.

Mom and Dad were quick to become evangelists when they adopted a new ideology, and would elucidate the benefits of home birth, geodesic domes, or debt-free living, whenever given the opportunity.

Janet, the midwife, came for several visits prior to the delivery. When the time was right for the auspicious event, my sisters and I were shuffled off to spend the night with our cousins. Immediately upon our return home early the next morning, May 13th, 1984, we were euphoric to discover the arrival of a baby brother.

My sisters and I instantly fell in love with Cameron Dare, the name my parents gave to the newest member of the family. We eagerly took turns holding him while Mom and Dad called family members to announce the birth.

Grandma and Grandpa Summers happily received the news, but were confused. They talked to my mom first, and then to me and Adrienne. We grasped the phone between us, and leaned our heads in close.

"Are you excited to have a new baby brother?" Grandpa asked us.

"Yeah!" we exclaimed in unison.

"Are you at the hospital?"

"No, we're at home," answered Adrienne.

"Are your mom and the baby there?"

"Yes," I responded.

"How did they get home so fast?" Grandpa persisted.

"I don't know," I replied.

Adrienne and I could both sense that something wasn't right. We wanted off the phone and out of the conversation.

Grandpa told us to get Dad on the phone. After a brief exchange between the two men, all hell broke loose. Dad confessed that the baby had been delivered at home, whereupon Grandpa shouted an angry retort before disconnecting at his end of the line.

"He hung up on me!" Dad bellowed, staring in disbelief at the telephone in his hand.

Two and a half hours later, Grandpa's Buick pulled into our driveway. This was quite a trick, considering it should have taken three hours to drive from their home in Utah. We heard first one car door close, and then the loud slam of the second. The girls and I hastily retreated to the far end of the trailer house, although there is no privacy in a mobile home when someone starts yelling.

"What in the hell do you think you are doing!?" Grandpa shouted at my dad as he entered the front door. "Elaine might be your wife, but she's my daughter. How dare you risk her life!"

"We decided together to do this," Mom protested.

Grandpa wasn't having any of it. He was in a shouting frame of mind, and was not about to listen to anyone's reasoned logic regarding the hot topic at issue.

"Listen you sonofabitch," Grandpa growled, "what gives you the right?"

Though we couldn't see what was going on, in my mind's eye I envisioned my Grandpa with his six-foot-two frame towering over my father, their faces just inches apart.

I couldn't hear Dad's reply, but I did hear Grandma beseeching her husband to calm down.

"Jess," she said, "Jess, this isn't doing any good."

I can picture her holding my new brother in her arms, gently swaying from side-to-side, earnestly trying to restore peace and order amidst the chaos.

Soon Grandpa had calmed down somewhat, and my sisters and I left our safe retreat to greet our grandparents. The situation was too awkward with heightened emotion to accommodate everyone cramped together in the trailer's tiny living room, so Grandma and Grandpa left our home not ten minutes after their arrival. They drove into central Burley to stay at my great-grandma's house.

Although Dad and Grandpa eventually returned to civil relations, some things can never be unsaid. This was not to be the last time Grandpa and Dad would clash over ideas and ideals. Grandpa was already doubtful regarding both Dad's choice to pursue art as a career, and his decision to build the dome. It was almost inevitable that an open clash would happen at some point, and a home baby delivery provided the perfect tinder to ignite the first major confrontation.

Dynamic Duo

As Dad's career in art continued to unfold, it became increasingly clear he couldn't succeed without my mother's help. Although Dad had natural talent, and his artistic skill was swiftly developing, Mom was the born salesperson, promoter, and businesswoman.

My mother was also a supreme optimist. Cheerful to a fault, she believed that she could do anything if she set her mind to it and maintained a positive attitude. I remember Mom reading a wide range of sales books by such authors as Zig Ziglar, Spencer Johnson, and Brian Tracy, together with Norman Vincent Peale's *Power of Positive Thinking*. In spite of the many challenges she and my dad faced, Mom was perpetually pragmatic and sanguine, traits that served to counterbalance my father's tendencies to brood and despair.

As Dad continued painting, and Mom honed her prowess in selling art at Lightworks, they realized that together they had real potential to succeed. They could ultimately see that their best sales promise was not to local buyers through their own gallery, but rather through established galleries in larger art markets. Their professional vistas were growing ever more expansive.

Now that they were showing in Boise and Burley, and Dad had been able to paint a sufficient number of paintings to have a substantial inventory, it was time to approach additional galleries.

Dad's first venture was to Portland, Oregon. He had helped a friend move from Burley to the Seattle area, and then borrowed her old rusted-out station wagon to drive some of his art down to Portland.

The art scene was significantly different in Portland from Boise or Burley. Though there were landscape painters represented in some of the galleries, the primary focus of the Portland market was Northwest tribal art. Dad struck out in a number of galleries in which the owners felt Dad's mountain scene and still-life work weren't a fit.

Dad doggedly persisted, however, and continued to visit the dwindling list of galleries he had compiled from the phone book.

It was late in the afternoon when he visited the Quintana Gallery. There was initially nothing about the gallery that indicated it would be a good fit for Dad's art. The primary focus, like that of so many other Portland galleries he had visited, appeared to be on local and native art.

Cecil, the owner, was a gregarious man in his late forties. He immediately struck up a conversation with my dad, and the two of them hit if off. Cecil agreed to look at Dad's portfolio, and when Dad offered to show him some actual work, he readily assented.

"Where is it?" the gallery owner asked.

"I have some pieces out in the car," Dad replied, making his way to the door.

"I'll come with you!" Cecil exclaimed.

"It's alright, I can get it and bring it in," Dad said, now in a bit of a panic.

"Nonsense," Cecil insisted, "I'll help you."

Perhaps Cecil didn't want Dad traipsing into the gallery with a lot of artwork while they were trying to conduct business. It would also be easier to dismiss Dad out at the car if he wasn't interested in the art.

Dad couldn't refuse, but any hope he had of portraying himself as a successful, established artist would now be impossible. Though the station wagon Dad had borrowed managed to make it from Burley, Idaho, to Seattle, Washington, and then on down to Portland, Oregon, it was not a pretty sight to behold.

Mr. Quintana had every reason to be legitimately impressed with the quality of Dad's work and the extent of his talent, but I'm not entirely sure that his agreeing to represent Dad wasn't also driven by a smattering of pity. Whatever his motivation, the Horejs family owes Cecil Quintana a debt of gratitude.

The Quintana Gallery proved to be one of the most important galleries in Dad's early career. Despite the fact that Dad's art wasn't their usual fare, the gallery staff came to love and respect my mom and dad, and to sell a lot of Dad's work to their collectors. More importantly, the gallery served as a credibility booster and confidence builder for Dad, which he and my mother leveraged to open gallery doors in other markets.

By this point in his career, Dad had traded his Lincoln for a long, green Dodge van. The van's considerable length accommodated three rows of bench seats for the kids, plus cargo space to haul a goodly number of paintings. Because the back seats could be removed, and because my parents, along with most other parents at the time, viewed seatbelts as optional, the van was flexible, and proved perfect for traveling long distances to present Dad's work to galleries.

During the years Mom and Dad pursued their quest to expand their representation, I remember a particular gallery trip to Salt Lake City. Mom and Dad systematically approached all of the galleries they could find in the phone book. They had put together a portfolio with snapshots of Dad's art, which they presented to the gallery owners they met.

Mom did most of the talking when they entered a gallery, extolling the virtues of her husband's art. A conversation would ensue, and if the gallery owner was interested, Mom and Dad would return to the van to retrieve the actual paintings, which they would then show the owner.

At least that's what I understood was happening. All of the kids would stay in the van (another indication of how different the times were) growing more and more impatient as the day wore on.

After several gallery visits, the owner of a small gallery downtown took a liking to Dad's work and agreed to show it in his space, which was both gallery and frame shop, much like my parents' Lightworks Gallery. This small success was clear evidence of the potency of Mom's positive thinking, and confirmed the importance of persistence when approaching galleries.

Dad developed a new way of presenting his work as his business evolved. In the beginning years, he framed his work in traditional wood or gold-leafed frames, as most landscape artists did. In fact, one of the advantages of having the frame shop in Lightworks Gallery was that it allowed him to frame his own work at wholesale prices.

However, his vision for the presentation of his work changed while visiting Seattle on a gallery-hunting trip in the early eighties. While there, Dad met an artist who was stretching his own canvases on two-inch-deep wood boxes. This artist was using painter's tape to mask the edges of the canvas so that when the artwork was finished, he could remove the tape, leaving a clean border around the painting.

The artwork was then hung without a frame, the border serving to set off the image from the wall.

Dad noted that the Seattle artist was painting abstract imagery, but liked what he was doing with the borders, and realized that he could incorporate the same approach into his art to achieve a more contemporary look for his landscapes. The artist generously shared his techniques for building the stretchers; because Dad was painting landscapes, the abstract painter didn't view Dad as a competitor.

Dad returned to his studio and began developing his own version of the stretched and bordered canvases, thus revolutionizing the look of his work. This new presentation would become a hallmark of his paintings, and the manner in which he would present all of his art from that point forward.

Perhaps Mom and Dad's other rebellions against norms had prepared Dad to buck the painting and framing establishment as well. This new approach to presenting his work would, over the course of the years, save Dad tens of thousands of dollars in framing costs—an additional incentive for making the change.

DAD FLEES TO BRAZIL

In February of 1986, Dad had an unexpected break from the gallery, the dome, and from Burley. The local chapter of the Rotary Club had been looking for someone to send to Brazil, and the someone they were commissioned to send needed to be of cultural interest and substance. Burley, suffering from the aforementioned lack of culture, provided slim pickings in the population from which the Rotarians must choose. As fortune would have it, a member of the club remembered the Lightworks Gallery and Dad's artwork, and put his name forward. When Dad said he would be willing to go, his nomination was ratified and plane tickets were purchased.

Dad bought a Berlitz course in Portuguese, and began a crash course to teach himself the language. His fluency in French likely made the task easier, and with his new grasp of the basics of Portuguese, he set off in February for the nearest international airport, which was three hours away in Salt Lake City. He was primed and ready for the adventure. He would be in Brazil for six weeks.

One can only imagine what my mother thought. We still had a gallery to run, finances were always tight, and while Dad was taking his camera to capture images that could provide the fodder for future paintings, he wasn't going to be getting much painting done while he was traveling. Mom would have to rely on the sales of existing inventory to sustain herself and the five of us children.

To cap off the extensive list of her concerns, Mom was expecting a sixth child with a mid-April due date. Dad wouldn't be flying back into the country until the nineteenth of April, thus leaving her to endure the risks of childbirth on her own if she went into labor prior to his return.

Dad flourished on his trip. He easily acclimated to the culture, customs, and language, and cultivated friendships in the city of Curitiba that would endure for years and enrich his life. He managed to paint a few small paintings while he was there, and took hundreds of photographs.

We talked to Dad a couple of times on brief and expensive international phone calls. Mom updated him on how things were going at home, and shared the details of her progressing pregnancy.

The six weeks went by quickly for him, but slowly for us. We tried to imagine what Dad was doing, and to divine what Brazil was like, scrutinizing every detail in the postcards he sent us.

It is a testament to Mom's fortitude that she never let worry consume her during Dad's absence, and maintained a routine that normalized the situation for us kids. It is a witness to her monumental willpower that her due date came and went without the hint of a contraction.

Okay, it's not that she couldn't have had the baby without my dad there; she and the midwife would have been fine. The fact of the matter was that she wanted the birth to be a shared experience, and when Elaine Horejs sets her mind to something, that something comes to be.

Dad flew back, arriving in Salt Lake City on Saturday, April 19th. My brother, Graydon, was born in Burley on the following Saturday, April 26th. He weighed in at a hefty 9 lbs, 10 oz, a result, no doubt, of all the waiting Mom had him do so that his father could be home for the blessed event. Dad has always joked that Graydon was born three months old.

The Demise of Lightworks Gallery

As the sales of artwork increased through the various galleries where Dad was showing, he came to understand that he couldn't afford to spend his time framing or teaching art classes; he needed to be in the studio creating. Though the family's gallery was making some money, Mom was too busy raising us kids to continue spending regular workday hours in the gallery. Between creating his art and building the dome, Dad, too, was finding it more and more difficult to manage the Lightworks enterprise.

So they sold it.

When a local woman who had become a client and a friend expressed interest in owning the gallery, my parents jumped on the opportunity. A modest price was agreed upon, and Dad consented to carry on working in the gallery for a few months to teach the new owner how to operate the business.

I was too young to understand exactly what was happening, and the significance of the sale was beyond me. I do remember there being some tension after the purchase had gone through. The new owner lacked the disposition and savvy to operate a retail business: thus, it wasn't long before the gallery was in financial jeopardy.

Dad and Mom tried to help the beleaguered captain right the ship, but it was soon clear that captain and ship were foundering. Within a few short months, Lightworks Gallery closed its doors for good.

The gallery's demise marked the end of a brief cultural glimmer in Burley's otherwise spartan aesthetic landscape. Its sale and subsequent closing, though sad for Burley, did have an efficacious impact upon Dad's career: he was now able to spend more time painting. The financial consequences were less encouraging. The gallery had provided a modest cash flow, and now that it was gone, our family's fortunes depended entirely on the fickle winds of art sales.

Dad had been using the back room of the gallery as a studio. Now that the gallery was gone, he needed to find a new place in which to paint. The dome, being fully enclosed and almost watertight at this point, was the obvious choice. Even though the structure was nowhere near finished, setting up his studio in the dome made good sense. Dad could avoid the expense of renting a studio space in town, and could readily transition from painting to construction, and back again.

This plan worked out pretty well during the late spring, through the summer, and into the fall. The plan was less effective during the winter. Even though the concrete and foam outer shell of the dome offered protection from the wind and snow, the structure offered no thermal insulation for the retention of heat.

Dad set up his easel and palette on a concrete slab in the middle of the dome. He ran an extension cord from the trailer to power electric lights. He utilized a propane heater in an effort to stave off the bitter cold, to little effect. When temperatures dropped into the twenties, teens, and lower, no amount of heat from the space heater could beat back the icebox cold that permeated the interior of the dome.

While the dome lacked sufficient sealing to keep in heat, the plastic sheeting on the windows had the capacity to trap moisture. The humidity level in the dome was high, meaning that not only was Dad painting in a cold environment, he was painting in a cold, damp environment. Condensation on the plastic sheeting constantly dripped, or froze solid. The whole situation was miserable, verging on intolerable.

Dad bundled up in long underwear, wool pants, multiple shirts and coats, and donned a wool cap, ear muffs, and gloves. Not the typical garb of an artist, and certainly not the clothing conducive to the dexterity required by an impressionist painter.

Many artists suffer for their art, but during those long, cold winter days, Dad went through incredible hardships in order to create. Not surprisingly, the physical suffering began to take its toll, and Dad became increasingly cranky and dolefully depressed, a pattern that would repeat every winter, even when circumstances were not so dire.

A Momentous Christmas

Like most parents, Mom and Dad loved to surprise us at Christmas, but being that the holidays were invariably a time of constricted cash flow, they were unable to shower us with gifts. We were not the family that had all of the latest and greatest toys and gadgets. On Christmas morning, my sisters, brothers, and I might each have two or three small gifts, and find a few additional packages under the tree that were intended for the family to enjoy together.

One year we couldn't afford a Christmas tree. Dad found a large tumbleweed, spray-painted it silver, and strung it with lights. Beside posing a fire risk, our tumbleweed Christmas tree was a dismal reminder of how tight our family finances had become.

Looking back today, I realize that none of that really mattered one iota. As children, we found Christmas mornings magical, and thoroughly enjoyed the few presents we did receive. I don't recall any feelings of holiday deprivation during my early years. I do remember responding with a smidgen of incredulity when certain of my schoolmates recounted the specifics of their enormous Christmas hauls. I can look back at the young boy I was then, and tell him that what he had going for him was worth more than all the presents money could buy.

There was one particular Christmas when the gifts seemed unusually sparse. We opened the few presents placed under the tree within a few minutes. While we sat contemplating our new toys, Dad's voice caught our attention.

"It looks like there's something else under the tree. I think you might have missed something."

Sure enough, there, under the tree, was an envelope. Adrienne opened the envelope and found a single sheet of unlined paper with a note that directed us to look under the piano.

Wait. What piano?

As difficult as it may be to believe, my parents had managed to move a baby grand Kimball piano into the living room of the mobile home. They traded art for the piano to have it in the gallery, and when they sold the gallery, they kept the piano. Since we didn't have anywhere to store it until it could be moved into the dome, it found its way into the trailer, where it occupied more than half of the living room.

This wouldn't have been so bad, but by this time there were seven of us living in a two bedroom trailer. This meant that the three girls were in one bedroom, my baby brother Cameron and I were in the second bedroom, and my parents were sleeping on a hide-a-bed sofa in the living room. With the grand piano. None of us played the piano. But there it was.

Okay, so that Christmas morning we had the note that informed us there was something under the piano. All of the children scrambled over to the piano and found an old blanket covering a cardboard box. After a minute or two of wrestling to open the box, we found a television.

A television!

Our very own television!

Dad helped us pull the television out of the box and set it up. The screen wasn't huge, but the clunky, wood-sided box covering the picture tube was. Rabbit-ear antennas projected out of the top.

We turned the television on and were greeted by static. Turning the dial to change the channel, we found more static, until we reached channel eleven; channel eleven burst into glorious color and sound. Channel eleven was a CBS affiliate that broadcast out of Twin Falls, and was the only station we could receive over the air. There was no cable available in the countryside where we lived; thus if we were to have had a full range of television stations, we would have had to purchase a satellite dish. In those days, a dish was eight to ten feet in diameter, costing several thousand dollars. There was no way our family was going to come up with that kind of money. We had to be happy with our one, lonely, local channel. And we were. We were elated!

A diary entry in my journal from that period will illustrate how important television quickly became in my daily life.

2/2/85

I got up at about 7:30 to watch cartoons. Then we played. At 3:00 I helped clean up the house. Then I played. At 6:00 we watched "Otherworld" At 7:00 I watched "Difirent Strokes" At 7:30 I watched "Double Trouble" At 8:00 I watched "Gimme a Break" At 8:30 I watched "It's Your Move" At 9:00 I watched "Cover Up." At 10:25 I went to bed.

For several years, my journal entries read like the TV Guide.

Although we had our favorite shows, we would watch anything and everything that came on channel 11; since there was only the one option, we didn't waste our precious hours channel surfing. We didn't have a remote control for the tv, and we didn't need one. On or off were our options, and whenever possible, we chose on.

From Bad to Worse

In the fall of 1986, our family took a break from the mobile home. My great-grandparents Poulton, Dad's mother's parents, built a small home in Burley, and had lived there as long as I could remember. Great-grandpa Poulton had recently passed away, and his wife, Mary, my great-grandma, was too frail to take care of herself. The family moved her into a nursing home in Twin Falls, leaving the house in Burley vacant.

During the interim of time the extended family took to decide what to do with the house, Mom and Dad offered to move our family into the home and clean it, spruce it up, and maintain it through the winter. Because the home was still partially furnished, we moved only a few of our belongings in and set up house.

This was a momentous change for the Horejs family. Suddenly we were in a normal house with solid brick walls, four bedrooms, and a basement. The property had a real yard with grass, which I was assigned to mow. I absolutely loved mowing that grass, and did so one day a week after school, without being prompted, right up until the weather got cold enough that the grass fell dormant.

Dad set up a studio in the basement, which, in contrast to the dome, was well-heated, allowing him to paint throughout the winter without the threat of freezing.

I also discovered that the television in the basement was still hooked up to cable television. Mom and Dad would never have paid for cable. Apparently we were in the grace period of the former subscription, which meant that for a few weeks we had a vast array of programming from which to choose. Paradise!

I was in the sixth grade at the time, and it happened that Mountain View Elementary, where all of the fifth and sixth graders in the district went to school, was two blocks away from the house. I didn't even have to ride the bus to get to school—how fortunate for me!

Everything would have been perfect were it not for the fact that during the winter, for the first time I remember, our family completely ran out of money. There had been many times when funds were tight, but this was different. None of Dad's galleries were managing to sell anything through that winter, and we no longer had the small income from Lightworks Gallery. There was no other ready source of cash.

My sisters and I first noticed that something was wrong when the tension began to rise between Mom and Dad. There was an edge in both their voices whenever they spoke to one another, and we frequently heard them talking late into the night in their bedroom.

Mom stopped going to the grocery store, and suddenly we were drinking reconstituted, powdered milk instead of the real stuff, and we were eating oatmeal and Cream of Wheat for breakfast. We were taking sack lunches to school every day, until Mom could no longer afford to buy a loaf of bread—that's how bad the situation became.

Our only salvation was that Grandpa Horejs had given us a case of bottled peaches, harvested from his small fruit orchard. I recall waking up to eat peach cobbler for breakfast. With a note from my mom, I would be excused from lunch at school, and walk home to eat more cobbler. I can scarcely recollect what we ate for dinner during that period, but I do remember going to bed many nights with a gnawing emptiness in my stomach, and a fear of the future in my head.

Not only was there no money, worse still, there was no real prospect of any immediate relief. Even if artwork were to sell, there was always a delay between the sale and the gallery's sending of the check for my dad's commission. It seemed entirely possible to me that Dad might never sell another painting, and that we would all perish for want of food.

When one gallery finally called and let Mom know that a small painting had sold, she was compelled to ask if there were any possibility they could accelerate the payment, as we were in dire circumstances. That must have been a difficult task for her.

Because the galleries all sent payment by mail, and because those payments were so important to us, the mailbox had become, and would remain throughout my childhood, a kind of mystical shrine. Every day, sometimes several times a day, Mom or Dad, or one of the children would check the box to see if the mail gods had delivered a much prayed and hoped for check.

When the small check arrived that winter, the relief was fleeting. Mom, the family's chief financial officer, had to decide which bills to pay in a challenging allocation of funds. A trip or two was made to the grocery store, and in a few days' time, the money was gone, and the grinding desperation returned.

Mom might have called her parents, and Dad his, for loans, but there were limits as to how much could be borrowed from my grandparents. My grandma and grandpa

Summers were likely still upset that Mom and Dad chose to have a second child, my brother Graydon, at home. They also must have wondered why Dad wouldn't just man-up and get a real job, rather than continuing to pursue his crazy dream of becoming a genuine artist, capable of supporting his family with brushes and paint.

Our church would have been able to provide assistance with food and finances as well; however, I don't remember our receiving that kind of aid. I don't know whether Mom and Dad were too proud to ask, or whether they were justifiably convinced that church leaders would have sternly counselled Dad to find a paying job.

Even now, thirty years after that winter, writing about that difficult time brings tears to my eyes. The sense of despair and hopelessness that filled my great-grandparents' brick house that winter was pervasive. The dire straits in which we found ourselves looked to be inescapable. I was old enough at that point to know what was going on, and young enough to be powerless to change it. For the first time in my life, I wondered if my parents were going to fail to take care of us. The fear I felt was profound, and settled itself deep in my gut.

Eventually the new year came. Artwork began to sell. Money trickled through the mailbox, and into the bank account. The desperation lifted, though the worst was yet to come.

BUCKET BRIGADE

While we were living in town over that long winter of 1986-1987, disaster struck our temporarily-abandoned mobile home. Dad had dutifully drained all of the pipes in the house to prevent them from freezing. Either he didn't do a thorough job, or somehow an amount of water sufficient to cause havoc entered the pipes, froze, and burst the supply lines.

When my great-grandparents' home sold in the spring of 1987, we returned to the trailer. Dad turned on the water main line, whereupon we discovered that water was flooding from underneath the house, through the ruptured pipes.

Much cursing ensued.

Apparently the damage was extensive, and we were advised that it would cost many hundreds of dollars for a plumber to replace the water lines. One might have reasoned that having running water in the house was a top priority—a necessity even. Well, that would be true of most people.

My parents, however, looked at the problem in a different light. The construction of the dome, an eight month project now in its eighth year, was finally far enough along that an end was in sight. Diverting funds to repair the pipes on the trailer house would serve to delay construction. A decision had to be made. Dad and Mom decided to go for broke and finish the dome.

Though we didn't have running water inside the trailer, there was a water spigot just outside the pumphouse in back. It was still intact, so Dad hooked up a hose to the spigot and ran it into the trailer through the bathroom window. With a twist valve on the hose, we could fill up buckets and distribute water through the house as needed.

Fortunately, we had a ready supply of buckets. Dad had recently finished coating the outside of the dome in canvas (of course, what else would an artist use to seal a structure?), and painting it a stormy grey. We had stacks of empty, black, five-gallon paint buckets sitting around. We meticulously picked the layer of dried paint out of the buckets, and proceeded to use them to convey water.

Health experts might have protested that these buckets were not food-grade, but we did not let that bother us; the buckets were handy, and we needed to haul water around. It was only a few days before the residual paint flecks disappeared from our drinking and cooking water altogether.

Like many other children of the day, we siblings had a chore chart that included setting the table, clearing the table, washing the dishes, and taking out the trash. Adrienne and I also took turns hauling buckets of water from the bathroom to the kitchen: a chore I would wager was unique to our family.

One doesn't realize how much water it takes to supply a household, until one has to manually carry every ounce of that water in a bucket. Each morning we would fill the cleanest of the buckets (that is to say the one with the fewest microscopic remnants of paint), take it to the kitchen, and set it on the counter to supply our drinking water. We also brought in a bucket for cooking, and another for cleaning.

Water was scooped out of these buckets with a ladle or a pitcher.

To heat the water for cleaning, we filled a pan on the gas range and waited for it to begin to steam. The same large pan also held the water we heated to bathe. Several pans full of water were needed for a bath, and we learned to modulate the temperature to provide water warm enough to last an entire bath, yet never so hot that it would scald. From the stove, we hauled the pan of water back to the bathroom, and placed it in the tub. We used a plastic cup to pour the water over our heads, lathered up with soap, and poured more water over our heads and bodies to rinse.

Another bucket was left in the bathroom to catch the drips from the hose nozzle, which had a tendency to leak. This bucket would then be used to flush the toilet. All one had to do was pour adequate water into the mouth of the open toilet to trigger the flushing mechanism, and all was well.

Mom would use the hose to fill up the washing machine to start a load of wash. Our whites became a little dingy because heating and hauling water for the purpose of laundry was too onerous a task. Therefore, our loads of light, medium, and dark, were all washed in water of one temperature: ice cold, and straight from the well.

Adrienne and I made it a contest to see who could carry the most water. A five gallon bucket full of water would have weighed over forty pounds. I was thirteen, but scrawny, meaning that when the bucket hauling was initiated, I strained to carry a bucket three-quarters full. Within a few months, however, I was able to fill the bucket as close to the top as it could get without sloshing water when I carried it. Soon I discovered that, though twice as heavy, it was actually easier to carry two full buckets, one in each hand, because it provided balance.

In other words, we made do.

I'm not making any of this up.

That summer, a friend from church came over to play. It was a bright, sunny day, and we spent hours in the yard waging war against invisible enemies. As the day wore on and the temperature rose, we became thirsty.

"Can I have a drink?" my friend asked.

"Yeah, let me go get you one," I replied.

I ran up the steps and into the trailer. I found two glasses and dipped water out of the drinking bucket. The water was still cool, and was crystal clear. I returned to my friend, handed him a glass, and we both drank.

"Is it true you guys don't have running water?" he asked, handing me his empty glass.

I could feel my face turning bright red, and tears stung the corners of my eyes. A shy and sensitive kid, I was easily embarrassed. Having advanced in my reading beyond my peers, I was keenly aware of how the rest of the world lived, and how different my family was. It was humiliating that there were six children in the family, and that we were living in a mobile home: the lack of running water was too much to bear. I hung my head in shame.

"Yeah, it's true," I finally replied, a catch in my throat.

"How do you get water?" my friend continued, oblivious to my state.

"We have a hose."

"Why don't you fix the water?" he persisted.

"We're finishing the dome," I said, clutching both glasses and turning to take them back to the trailer's kitchen. "Mom and Dad don't want to spend the money to fix it when we're so close to finishing the dome."

I'm not sure if this answer satisfied him, since we didn't talk about it anymore. What bothered me most about the exchange was that it was clear my friend had heard about our situation from someone else. Had he heard it from his parents? Were adults talking about my family? Did the entire community gossip about the lack of running water in the Horejs's trailer?

It nearly killed me to think about all those people yammering about how poor we must be to not have running water in our home. I mean, wasn't our living in a tin house mortifying enough, without people laughing among themselves?

"How do you suppose they flush?"

CAR TROUBLE

Plumbing wasn't the only place we economized. Dad wouldn't pay for plumbers, and he wouldn't pay for mechanics unless he absolutely had to.

I don't know that Dad was particularly mechanically-minded. He was not the type of guy who, as a teenager, was tearing apart cars to rebuild them as hotrods. Nevertheless, he had picked up some notion of how engines worked from his father. He knew what was going on under the hood, and how to fix the most basic of problems that might cause a car to break down. It always seemed as though these problems cropped up when we could least afford to fix them. Consequently, Dad did a lot of the work himself.

We didn't have a garage, so I remember seeing Dad, time and again, sprawled out in the dust underneath his Lincoln, or later the van. Wrenches would be scattered in the driveway, and Dad would be cranking a tool or shaking the car to free one or another of the engine's parts. All the while, the disgruntled mechanic kept up his incessant cursing.

When I was old enough, I became mechanic's assistant, and handed Dad the tools he needed as he replaced a belt, a hose, a radiator, or an alternator. Thus did I gain a rudimentary understanding of the workings of an automobile. Few of these projects came off perfectly. We would often have to get additional parts from the auto-supply store, or call on a friend who knew a bit more about motors. Our cars were not above pooping out in the middle of winter, which added another dimension of torture to the repair process. Dad's frozen hands made it harder for him to fit parts, and easier for him to swear at the car.

I've never sought professional analysis: be that as it may, I'm pretty confident I have a certifiable neurosis with regard to car trouble, stemming from these traumatic repair sessions.

THE BIG ONE

In the fall of 1986, Dad received one of the biggest art projects of his burgeoning career. The gallery owner in Boise was working with First Interstate Bank to help them furnish their Boise headquarters with art. The bank wanted something that was illustrative of Idaho, and they needed a large painting. The gallery owner proposed Dad, among other artists he represented, to receive the commission for the project. Dad was selected!

Dad chose a mountain lake from the Sawtooths as his subject, and set about to build a huge canvas. He had done other large paintings using his tape-bordered, box-stretched canvases, by creating multiple panels, wherein the scene transitioned from one panel to the next. This project required him to build one massive, intact stretcher, five feet tall and eight feet wide.

As was usual under Mom's urging, Dad attacked the project with gusto. He spent long hours devising the engineering of the wood frame that would underpin the canvas. He had to buy a special bolt of canvas that was sufficiently long and wide to cover the stretchers. The painting itself required massive amounts of oil paint.

Then, once the piece was finished, there was the challenge of transporting it.

Our family had recently replaced the ancient Dodge van with a blue Chevy custom van. This van had it all: captain's chairs in the front and middle, a fold down bench across the back that turned into a bed, plush carpet, and a built-in sink and cooler.

For a family of seven, this was an ideal way to travel. On long trips, we blatantly disregarded safety as the children undid their seatbelts and sprawled in every direction. Three small kids could sleep on the back fold-down bed, while two older kids could recline in the captain's chairs. Should we happen to have an additional passenger, a family friend or cousin, one child could sleep on the floor beneath the back bench, and another could sleep in the aisle between the middle seats. The blue van was a veritable sleeping machine!

The problem with the van was that all of that seating, together with the sink and cooler, limited cargo space. When necessary, Dad folded down the back bench and stacked it with paintings. He placed a large painting along the tops of the middle seats, where it rested between the chair backs and the headliner (this required the children in the middle seats to spend the journey ducking and slouching in the chairs to avoid bumping their heads against the painting). The more artwork Dad stacked, the fewer passengers he could fit.

In the case of the artwork going to Boise, these considerations were all moot because the painting was too large to fit through the back door of the van. Dad knew that renting a truck or trailer to get the painting to Boise would be costly. To save money, he improvised a box for the painting with cardboard and rope, and strapped it to the top of the van. Then he headed northwest on Interstate 84 on his way to become a bigshot artist.

The installations went well, the executives of the bank liked the painting, and a few weeks later, the largest check Dad had yet received for his artwork arrived in the sanctified box.

I have forgotten the precise numbers: the painting sold for twelve or thirteen thousand dollars, a sum of gargantuan proportion to my teenage sensibility, and especially appreciated, coming as it did after a prolonged period of privation.

The gallery kept half the money as their commission on the sale; even so, our bank account was suddenly flush. Many overdue bills were paid. Groceries were stocked, and our table was host to bounteous feasts. We enjoyed a few of the luxuries that had been missing for a while—extravagances such as haircuts, school lunches, and full tanks of gas.

As Dad's career continued in earnest, our lives became an ongoing cycle of feast or famine. Money might come in from a sale in Sun Valley, Jackson Hole, Boise, or Portland, and in later years from a gallery in Santa Fe or Scottsdale. For a few weeks everything would be fine and dandy. The expenses of a large family like ours, however, were constantly expanding, and incoming funds were rarely sufficient to make ends meet.

I remember Mom and Dad making plans to budget and better manage our allocation of funds, so as not to have stretches of impoverishment. No matter how much they planned, or how disciplined they commited to be, the cash from the last sale never quite got us through the desert to the next.

In desperation—or exasperation—Mom wisely began a strategy of storing commodities and foodstuffs, thus staving off starvation during the inevitable slumps in our income. Being Mormon in Southern Idaho meant that for us, home storage was a common practice among our fellow congregants.

Mormons believe strongly in provident living and food storage. The Church (capitalized—The Church—by the 70-80% of the local population who were adherents) had farms and orchards, and operated granaries, mills, and canneries to help the faithful prepare.

"Prepare for what?" you might ask.

I was never totally clear about the reasoning, but many church members believed, as did their leaders, that Jesus Christ's second coming would be preceded by chaos, calamity, and apocalypse. The only thing standing between the faithful and utter destruction would be their year's supply of food (in addition to their faith and prayers).

I wasn't sure when Jesus was coming back, but I did worry that he might arrive before Dad's next commission check. Large tin cans of dried minestrone soup, dehydrated fruits and vegetables, and powdered milk, together with buckets of whole wheat, rice, and beans, got us through many a drought in sales.

As part of our "provident living" regime, Mom bought a combination wheat grinder/mixer. She taught us how to pour the wheat kernels into the machine to produce finely powdered whole wheat flour. The bread she made was heavy, hearty, and delicious. At first my siblings and I complained about the bread, and longed for the fluffy white Wonder Bread we had consumed for years. Then we became accustomed to the dense bread and grew to enjoy the flavor. Ultimately, we asked for Mom's bread even when we were in the money.

Our weekly dinner menu became a kind of bellwether for the family's financial situation. If the food came mostly from our food storage, we knew things were tight; if it came from the grocery store, we figured there must be a few dollars in the account.

Dad's sale in Boise meant that we ate like royalty for a while, or at least like a normal family, and that the bills were paid on time. The water situation in the trailer wasn't improved, but work accelerated dramatically on the dome. This was a good thing, because Dad was now working under an ultimatum.

Mom had once again become pregnant in the spring of 1988. She let my dad know in no uncertain terms that we were to be moved into the dome by that fall. If not, we were going to scrap the project, once and for all, and move into a house in town. She wasn't going to give birth to her seventh child in the mobile home. She wasn't kidding. The final push was on.

CHILD LABOR LAWS DON'T APPLY HERE

Dad rousted us early on the day we were to learn to make concrete. It was a clear, bright morning, and though the sun was just peeking over the mountains in the east, the birds were already singing, and the cool of the dawn was retreating.

I rubbed sleep from my eyes, and made my way into the trailer's kitchen to eat a quick breakfast. I was still thirteen that summer. Adrienne, a year and a half younger, ate breakfast with me before we stumbled out into the driveway where Dad was already at work.

Like most kids, we weren't particularly fond of hard work, but learning to mix concrete was something new, and a process complex enough to be interesting. Dad had borrowed a small cement mixer from the equipment rental shop in town, and it stood off to one side of the dirt driveway, gleaming an orange-yellow, ready to work. Next to the mixer was a fresh pile of sand, and another of gravel, both having been dumped by trucks the day before. Alongside these piles was a pallet of rectangular cement bags.

"Alright," Dad said, "here's what you do. You take a bag of the cement . . ."

He grabbed one of the heavy bags of cement and dropped it on the ground, where it landed with a thud.

"Then you take your shovel and cut it open."

Gripping the shovel like a spear, Dad lanced it into the bag seven or eight times, cutting the face of the bag to open a large, letter "I" shaped hole. He bent over and grabbed the bag, hefted it up to the round mouth of the mixer, and dumped in the finely powdered cement.

"Then you get three buckets of sand," he continued.

Dad began shoveling sand into a short, black bucket. When it was full, he lifted the bucket to the mixer and poured in the sand. He repeated the process, pouring three more buckets of the grey sand into the opening of the orange mixer.

"And now," he said, "there is a little trick before you add a bucket of water: this ought to help keep the dust down."

He tipped the mixer up a bit, and squirted a fine spray from the hose all around the interior of the machine. He then filled the bucket with water from the hose.

Dad flipped the switch on the machine and the mixer began whirring, turning at a rapid, steady pace. Cement dust billowed from the mouth; Dad took a step back, which action Adrienne and I mimicked. After he sprayed more water to settle the dust, he put down the hose, picked up the bucket of water, and stepped forward to pour it into the mixer.

Now the mixer seemed to slow its rounds as the blend inside began to thicken. The three of us stood there, transfixed: oh, the wonder of it all! We felt mesmerized by the rhythmic revolutions of the spinning drum.

"This is the mortar mix," Dad explained, shaking himself free from the grip of his stupor. "John is going to use it to put the blocks together. We'll finish this batch, and then you should be able to mix three or four batches of the filler. You use three buckets of gravel in the filler, instead of sand;

otherwise, it's pretty much the same—one bag of cement, three buckets of gravel, and one bucket of water. Got it?"

Adrienne and I nodded mutely, and continued watching the first lot of concrete rotating in the mixer. The fresh concrete smelled earthy, and the whooshing sound as the mixture turned into usable mortar continued to soothe us.

It took about five minutes before Dad was satisfied with the mixture, and when he was, he grabbed the nearby wheelbarrow and rolled it next to the mixer. While the motor was still running, he grasped the handle on the side and tipped the mouth down over the wheelbarrow, letting the rich, grey mixture dump out. The wheelbarrow was nearly filled with the heavy cement. Dad tipped the drum back into position, grabbed the wheelbarrow, and rolled it across the driveway and on up the board ramp. We followed him and the wheelbarrow into the hulking dome structure, anxious to see how the mortar would be delivered to John, and how he would use it.

John Christiansen was already at work, laying out the cinder blocks we had been hauling into the dome for the last several days; he was fashioning a nearly circular pattern of blocks on the concrete footing in the center of the dome. Dad had hired John to help with the work this summer, as we had finally arrived at a point where there was skilled work to be done that Dad couldn't do himself.

With John hired, the work finally began to progress more quickly; he was an experienced construction worker, and knew how to get things moving. He was also a heavy drinker who had a hard time holding down regular employment.

This morning, John, a muscular, mustachioed man, had showed up pretty close to on-time, though his eyes were bloodshot, and his breath already smelled of alcohol. Getting to work seemed to cure his hangover, and he was glad to see Adrienne and me on the job site, ready with the first haul of mortar.

"You guys make me some mud?" he asked, eyeing the wheelbarrow.

He grabbed his trowel and scooped up some of the cement, letting it fall back into the barrow as he checked its consistency.

"Looks good," he said, "looks good."

Dad left the wheelbarrow with John, and the three of us walked back outside to the mixer.

"Let me see how you do," Dad said.

My sister and I gazed at one another, a blank look crossing our faces. The whole process was new enough that seeing it once wasn't enough to learn what to do.

"First grab a bag of the cement," Dad instructed, seeing that we weren't moving with any confidence.

Adrienne and I stepped to the pallet of cement, and each grabbed an opposite side of a bag to lift and toss to the ground. We strained considerably to do so. Each bag had its weight of eighty pounds printed on its face. I don't suppose I weighed more than a hundred pounds at the time, and I know I was still pretty scrawny, despite the hundreds of buckets of water I had carried over the last few months. Adrienne was smaller than I. It took considerable effort to move the bag, but we did manage to get it down.

Dad handed me the shovel, and just as he had done, I gripped it spear-like, and jabbed it into the paper that wrapped the cement. My first jab didn't manage to pierce the bag, glancing off the side. I put more momentum into my second thrust, making it through the paper and plastic lining of the bag. My cut was not straight, and my execution lacked Dad's confidence. It took me a full minute to open the face of the bag, and even then my opening was more of a mangling than a useful slit. I set the shovel aside, and Adrienne and I wrestled to lift the bag and dump its contents into the mixer, spilling only a smidgen into the dirt.

Now both of us began shoveling gravel into the bucket, as we had seen Dad do. Next we poured the contents of the bucket into the mixer, and then added a bucket of water.

This combination rumbled and grumbled in the mixer—the gravel clunking and clattering against the metal sides of the drum. The mixture needed a little more water, which we added from the hose.

After five minutes of mixing, the concrete was ready. There was only one wheelbarrow, and John was using that for his mortar; Dad directed us to grab a couple more buckets, and to set them under the mixer. We dutifully poured the first one nearly full of concrete. It was so heavy that neither Adrienne nor I could lift it, nor could the two of us manage it together.

Dad hauled this bucket into the dome, and we filled all subsequent buckets only half-full. Hauling water in the trailer had been the perfect way to condition ourselves for this job. At half full, we could half-drag-half-carry them, staggering into the construction site, where we poured the concoction into the cinder blocks that John was placing on the foundation.

The blocks were being stacked in a semicircle. Rebar protruded from the foundation. The blocks, each with two large holes, were placed in such a manner that the rebar extended upward through the holes to hold the blocks in place. John spread mortar beneath each block, pressed the blocks down into place, and dispensed with the excess mortar with his trowel.

We soon got into a rhythm. We alternately mixed mortar and concrete, and between batches, we hauled cinder blocks into the dome. Cinder blocks are lightweight, cubed bricks made from ash, sand, and cement. Each block measures 8 inches x 8 inches x 16 inches, and has a horizontal slab dividing the hollow interior. The blocks are stacked so that the right hole and left hole of a block on one row fit over the left hole and right hole of an adjacent block in the row below. The rebar lends strength and stability to the construction, and the cement poured in to fill the cores of the blocks dries and hardens to form incredibly sturdy walls.

Adrienne and I learned that a block, which when seen from above looks like a squared figure eight, is designed so that the sides and the center slab are thicker at the top, and then taper, thus making the block easy to grip by the top with one hand. We could grab one brick in each hand, and each of us haul two at a time into the dome.

All of the work was hard—very hard—for young teenagers. Our hands quickly blistered and bled, and our muscles throbbed in protest. I'm sure we complained about the work. However, our blisters slowly turned to callouses, and our hands eventually hardened. Our muscles grew taut. We loved being treated like grown-ups, entrusted with real responsibilities. Our resolve increased. Our pride in being part of the process that would make a dream come true was exhilarating. Someday, in the not too distant future, the Horejs family would make the dome their home.

The construction of the block wall in the center of the dome was progressing rapidly. Over the next several weeks, Adrienne and I helped Dad and John to build it up to the second story. We nailed together the joists in the ground level floor, covered them with plywood, and nailed the plywood into place.

In doing these tasks, we learned how to hold a hammer, and how to drive in a nail, while minimizing the risk of striking a thumb. We learned how to cut wood to precise measurements. We learned how to square joints.

Most importantly, we learned how to work hard.

The days were long, but rewarding. Nail by nail, and block by block, we were finishing the dome.

THE TWENTY-FOOT MOVE

By September, we were far enough along with construction to dare to believe we would soon actually move into the dome. All of the floors were completed, and the center tower now reached its final height of twenty-five feet. The interior walls were in place, though only a few were sheet-rocked. The others were "temporarily" covered in canvas.[3] Fixtures had been installed in the bathrooms, plumbing and electrical run, and a furnace set up in the crawl space beneath the center tower.

Dad had also replaced the plastic sheeting that first covered the window spaces with sheets of polycarbonate—the same transparent plastic used in the cockpits of fighter jets. Though Dad didn't anticipate a circumstance that might benefit from bullet-proofing our windows, he did appreciate the added protection against abrasion, impact, and UV exposure, and the bonus of effective thermal insulation. The material was perfect for the

---

[3] At the time of this writing, those "temporary" wall coverings have been in place for thirty years!

dome because it could be cut to shape with a skillsaw, and then bent into a frame to fit the odd geometrics of the dome.

When stepping into the dome, one now observed a structure resembling an actual house, rather than the interior of a cave. It looked as though our funds were going to get us through to move-in. Perhaps Mom would have child number seven in the dome, rather than in the trailer.

Just as she had demanded.

Mom was due to deliver the first week of December. We started moving our possessions from the trailer into our new home the last week of November. Would we be settled before another baby joined the family?

Oddly, I can't remember my first night sleeping in the dome. Nor can I remember the first time we turned on the water in the kitchen sink or the shower. Our having running water at long last would have been an occasion steeped in gratitude, and worthy of celebration.

I do remember, however, what it was like to see the last of our possessions moved out of the trailer house. The six months we had planned to spend in the trailer had stretched out into nine long years, and it had become the only home I really knew. I didn't exactly hate the trailer. Nonetheless, I wasn't going to miss the wind howling through the aluminum siding during the winter, the pilot light constantly going out in the gas furnace, or hauling water—I especially wasn't going to miss hauling water.

We didn't immediately move the trailer off the property. Instead, Dad turned it into a workshop in which to build and stretch canvases. He had been doing this in the dome, where the process created a lot of sawdust, so it made sense to keep it out of the living space. It was decided that his studio would remain in the dome.

We readily discovered certain quirks that came with living in a concrete-lined geodesic dome. The most noticeable was the acoustic oddity of the structure. Because there were few permanent walls, there was absolutely no acoustic privacy. Conversations and television programs were broadcast to the entire household. While all sound carried throughout the dome, there were particular spots from which one could hear every sound down to a whisper: sounds that originated in the flip spot on the opposite side of the house. Someone's mutter from fifty feet away sounded like it was spoken right into another's ear.

Because heat rises and air circulation was minimal, the upper levels were warm in the winters, while it was difficult to keep the ground floor from becoming uninhabitably cold. During the summer, the upper levels were almost unbearably hot, while the ground floor was a bit cooler.

Another climatic oddity was the condensation that formed on the windows during the winter. If the humidity was high enough, the dew point low enough, and the air cool enough, the windows fogged up and dripped incessantly, and we experienced a rainforest-like environment throughout the dome.

All this condensation during the winter led to another problem. The front door was a huge sheet of polycarbonate plastic that opened in one corner by flexing outward. This was never intended to be the permanent door; Dad planned to build a front entryway with a more traditional door. As with many of the dome-related plans, however, this never happened.

During the winter, the condensation on the front door dripped onto the door frame and produced a lot of moisture. On cold nights this moisture froze and sealed the front door shut.

We would often awaken to the sound of a hair dryer blowing and the striking of a hammer and chisel, as Dad labored to break up the ice that sealed shut the front door. Much cursing accompanied this ritual.

By my birthday in late November of that year, Mom was very close to delivering. There was some thought that my newest sibling might even be born on my birthday, but the day came and went without Mom going into labor.

About that time, Mom sat Adrienne and me down and extended a special invitation.

"Since you are both old enough," she said, "if you would like, you can help the midwife, and watch the baby's birth."

I must have looked quite stunned, because she quickly amended her invitation.

"You don't have to participate or observe. I just wanted to invite you if you feel comfortable."

Comfortable!? I had just turned fourteen: it's difficult to imagine that anything could have made me feel less comfortable. I had read enough to understand the basics of the birthing process; my mother, a Victorian at heart, had never told us anything about the birds and the bees or the miracle of delivery. I knew for a fact that I didn't want to have anything to do with it, not with any aspect.

"I'll think about it," I said.

Adrienne, eleven, enthusiastically responded that she would like to be there.

With the onset of labor on an evening in early December, it became clear that Mom and Dad hadn't made provision for the kids to go and stay with family or friends. We went upstairs to bed as things got progressively more serious. I did my best to fall asleep. This was not easy with the acoustic anomalies in the dome. Mom, Dad, Adrienne, and the midwife were all ensconced in Mom and Dad's room on the first floor, with every sound they generated being carried on waves throughout our abode.

I managed to fall asleep by the time my brother, Devon, was born. I don't remember hearing the midwife leave, though it was likely that Dad made a ruckus chipping ice from the door to let her exit when her work was done.

We were all excited the next morning to welcome the newest addition to the family. Fortunately for us, by this time we children had all dropped out of the public school system, and were able to spend the whole day with the new baby. We happily took turns holding and cuddling Devon, and fetching and carrying for Mom.

FIGHTING THE SYSTEM

Mom and Dad's mistrust of the public school system had deepened over the course of the years. Though Adrienne, Yvette, Shalece, and I had all enrolled in the local public schools after the Montessori school closure, Mom and Dad weren't happy about it.

I continued to do well academically through the fourth, fifth, and sixth grades. Nonetheless, I was discontented with my fifth grade teacher, Mr. Hendricks, who I thought was mean and unfair to our class. He gave us all a failing grade on a test if he caught any student/students talking during the exam. He lost his temper and yelled when students misbehaved. As a quiet, well-behaved kid, I had little patience for my classmates' misbehavior, and no tolerance whatsoever for Mr. Hendricks's loud and angry outbursts.

I complained to Mom and Dad, who took my complaints along with their concerns to the principal. The principal scheduled a meeting between my parents and my teacher, after which Mr. Hendricks grew to be friendly and solicitous toward me. He motioned me up to his desk to talk about assignments, and to discuss my answers to questions on quizzes. He asked me about my plans for the future. He let me go out to recess early: an odd demonstration of favoritism, since I would then wander around the empty schoolyard alone for ten or fifteen minutes, waiting for the rest of my schoolmates to be dismissed for the break. The other kids in my class thought I was a brown-noser, and obviously resented the extraordinary treatment I was receiving. I soon wished that I had kept my mouth shut. In hindsight, I have to wonder whether Mr. Hendricks was passively-aggressively punishing me, rather than trying to win me over and court my parents' favor. Whatever the case may have been, the man sadly lacked the requisite demeanor to be effective in the classroom.

Without reference to any list of specific complaints we had about the school, my parents simply wanted us out of the system. They were coming to believe that the government mandated school network was corrupt from top to bottom.

Mom and Dad had some friends who were part of the John Birch Society. Like their friends, my parents began following conspiracy theorists, who believed that the constitutional government of the United States had been taken over by an evil cabal that was working to enslave its citizens through taxation and welfare.

I could scarcely keep track of all of the plots that had been allegedly hatched to oppress the free people of the United States. Was it the Rothchilds or the Illuminati who were running the United Nations, and supplanting our freedoms with a New World Order? I can't remember now, but there was apparently a shadow conspiracy rising to oppress the free people, especially those citizens who believed in God.

This kind of conspiracy theory has always existed; however, the late eighties and early nineties comprised a particularly fertile time for the fringe elements in this country to trade on these ideas. The federal government played right into the storyline through the mishandling of the volatile situations at Ruby Ridge in northern Idaho, and the Branch Davidian siege in Waco, Texas.

Mom and Dad saw the public schools, even those in a little town like Burley, as State instruments of brainwashing. The more they talked to their like-minded friends, the more they wanted out of the system.

I should have enrolled in middle school in the fall of 1987, but instead, my parents decided we were going to homeschool, and kept us out of school that autumn. They ordered textbooks directly from the publishers, books that had been vetted by other homeschoolers and found to be safe from brainwashing content.

We also joined a local homeschool group that organized field trips and recreational activities for other homeschool students in the area—there were a good number of them. Not all of the homeschool families were homeschooling to escape a corrupt system, though many of them were.

While my brothers and sisters and I were nonplussed at all the conspiracy talk, we were thrilled not to have to go to school anymore. All of a sudden, we were free to sleep in. We found that we could finish our schoolwork in a few short hours, and then were free to do whatever we wanted for the rest of the day. It was a kid's dream come true!

It soon became evident that discipline and consistency were not to be features of our new schooling regime. Many days we would skip studying altogether, especially if we were going to be on the road with Mom and Dad delivering artwork to a show, or engaged in some other activity—and there were a lot of other activities. Even so, we slowly progressed through our textbooks, and I continued to read extensively. Since I had been testing at the twelfth grade level when I left school after the sixth grade, I didn't have a lot to lose in my changed circumstances.

I'm not sure my younger siblings were quite as lucky. They never had the experience of sitting in a classroom day after day, working steadily at lessons. Sure, it was a boring drag to do so, but it also taught me discipline, persistence, and time management.

There were other compensations beyond escaping the tedium of the public school paradigm. After launching into homeschool, our family had opportunities to gain practical knowledge that very few other children would ever experience.

I Join the Family Business

One of the benefits of having many hours free each day was that I was able to join the family business. Besides helping to build the dome, the other experience I most credit with teaching me the value of work was Dad demonstrating how to build his canvases, and then mentoring me in mastering the process.

When Dad sold Lightworks Gallery, he kept many of the framing tools he had acquired over the years, and those tools were well suited to a canvas stretcher production shop. By the time I was old enough to apprentice in this part of the business, the shop was set up in the now-abandoned mobile home. Dad spent a few minutes showing me how to measure the strips of plywood that he had ripped at the local lumberyard, a few more on how to cut them using the power miter saw, and lastly, how to fit the corners together using framing clamps.

That was it; my apprenticeship was over, and I was put to work.

Dad would give me a list of canvas sizes he needed, and I would set to work measuring, cutting, and assembling the stretchers. For a while, I was also tasked with stretching and stapling the canvas cuts to the stretchers. Soon, however, we found that Adrienne could do this work, and the two of us started our own assembly line.

I was paid ten cents per linear inch for each stretcher assembly I completed. This meant that a stretcher measuring thirty inches by forty inches would net me seven dollars. I kept track of all of the stretcher frames I built each week, turned in the bill to my mom, and watched as she wrote me a check.

It was a liberating affair to have my own funds. Though my earnings were regulated by Dad's production, he was at this point generating more sales, thus providing a steady demand for stretched canvases.

I spent some of my money on the typical things teenagers buy: fast food, books, cassette tapes, and later, CDs, video games, and movie tickets. Because my parents saw an opportunity to teach me budgeting, and to reduce expenses, they required that I allocate a portion of my income to purchase my own clothing and shoes.

I quickly learned the value of money and the wisdom of thrift, and thus managed to keep myself dressed. Fortunately, I didn't need an expansive or expensive wardrobe since I wasn't attending school. I felt a sense of pride providing for myself, and never resented the responsibility.

As I became more proficient at building stretchers, I worked quickly and produced a quality product. I also learned lessons about task management that have served me well throughout my life. I discovered that when I received a list of sizes that Dad wanted, I should immediately cut the wood for all of the stretchers, and then proceed to build them, one after the other. I ordered the sizes from largest and most complex, to smallest and most simple. By working on the most difficult projects first, things grew easier as I progressed. I've stuck with that strategy throughout my life, and it's always made it easier to accomplish complex tasks. I also learned to stick with a job until it's finished.

I appreciate that Dad was willing to entrust this work, work that was so important in his career, to a teenager. He could have built the stretchers much more quickly himself when he was first training me; instead, he was patient, and taught me how to fix mistakes and persist in the work.

I felt real satisfaction in seeing the finished artwork that was sent to the galleries, where it would be sold to wealthy and discerning collectors. I knew that my handiwork was essential to the final product.

ROAD TRIPS

Even before we left public school, my family was well-traveled. My parents wouldn't hesitate to pull us out of class for a few days to take a trip to Portland or Scottsdale. One of the main justifications for permanently taking us out of the school system was that Mom deemed it more valuable for us to travel and see the country and its historical sites and national parks than for us to sit in a classroom.

During our first autumn outside the education aggregate, we took an epic trip across the country when Dad was to be featured in a gallery show in Virginia, just outside of Washington, D.C. We drove the blue van three thousand miles, going out of our way to see historical sites, and to visit family along the way.

We visited Mormon historical sites in Missouri, Illinois, and Upstate New York. We saw Civil War battlefields in Virginia and Pennsylvania. We toured the monuments and museums in Washington D.C. I distinctly remember visiting Mark Twain's home in Hannibal, Missouri. Twain was a hero of mine, and I was particularly impressed to see Tom Sawyer's fence.

Though the drive was wearying, I was the type of kid who could spend long hours looking out the window, watching the countryside go by. This was really my only option on long trips, as I was also the type of kid who got carsick and threw up if I tried to read a book, play a game, or engage in some other activity while the car was moving.

I don't remember whether Dad's show in Virginia was a huge success—I think that he did sell some paintings. What I do know is that the trip left wonderful memories that are still cherished by our family.

We had other adventures. I remember a trip to Portland, Oregon, in particular. In addition to packing the van with our family members, we had two passengers from Brazil, who were visiting on vacation. With the interior space filled to capacity, Dad strapped a stack of paintings to the top of the van.

As we were driving across a desolate stretch of Interstate 84 west of Boise, there was a loud snapping sound. We all instantly turned as one to look out the back window of the van, where we watched in horror as large canvases flew through the air and crash landed on the blacktop.

"Shit!" Dad yelled as he slammed on the brakes.

Cars behind us swerved, braked hard, and laid on their horns.

We pulled off to the side of the road, and Dad turned on the hazard flashers. Dad, Mom, and I jumped out of the van, and ran to retrieve the canvases that were scattered helter-skelter over the freeway.

Miraculously, the canvases hadn't hit any of the vehicles behind us, and more miraculously yet, the vehicles hadn't run over any of the canvases.

We gathered the paintings and placed them next to the van, allowing traffic to resume flowing on the freeway. Dad strapped the paintings back to the top of the van.

When we arrived in Portland, Dad had some significant work to do to clean the canvases, which though scuffed and scraped, were mostly intact. We rented more trailers after that trip: live and learn.

Though there was nothing typical about my childhood or adolescence, I, like many of my friends, was beginning to feel teen angst, and looking for opportunities to rebel. I started listening to alternative rock music, and letting my hair grow long. I argued with my parents about religion and politics. As a homeschooler, there wasn't much likelihood of my becoming involved in tobacco, drugs or alcohol, so I had to make my battles where I could.

Sometimes Dad would invite me to join him alone, when he was driving to deliver artwork to a gallery, or heading out to take photographs of scenery, which would become the subject matter inspiration for future paintings. We would spend hours in the car discussing a myriad of subjects: the beginning of the universe, the likelihood of a supreme being, alien life, potential threats to the Constitution of the United States, or the ineptitude of posturing politicians.

I was pretty sure that I had developed my own opinions through my extensive reading and studying, but looking back, I can see that many of my positions were in juxtaposition to my dad's. If he believed in God, I found the idea of an almighty, omniscient creator, who worried Himself over the negligible choices and actions of such insignificant creatures as mere humans, to be highly suspect, perhaps even laughable.

If he thought that conspiratorial cabals had taken over the political parties and were plotting to overthrow our freedom, I said "hogwash", and argued that the political establishment was critical for fighting off communism, and leading us into a new and brighter future.

If Dad thought art was the path to freedom and beauty, I believed business was. I let Dad know that when I grew up, I was going to be a business executive, or an insurance salesman—anything other than an artist. I wanted to have a nine-to-five job, a house with a white picket fence, and 2.5 children who would attend public school.

Oh yes, I was quite the rebel!

As time went on, I became more and more embarrassed by the vast and seemingly ever-growing size of our family. I was innately shy, and the looks our family would get as the nine of us traipsed into a restaurant were mortifying.

I remember a gallery owner expressing surprise when he learned that Mom and Dad had seven children.

"You need to buy a television!" he laughed.

I thought it odd that Mom and Dad didn't reply that we finally had one; when I figured out what he meant, I blushed profusely.

Dad invited me to attend some gallery openings with him, when I was old enough to have my driver's license and spell him behind the wheel. My perception of my father began to change during these father-and-son excursions.

In Portland, I was invited to go to dinner with my dad and the gallery's owner and staff before the art show and sale. I was included in the conversation at the table, and observed how much everyone liked my dad. He had an affable way about him, and an interest in the people he met. They would ask him questions about his art, and after responding, he would ask them questions about themselves and their interest in art.

That dinner in Portland was the first time I remember seeing my dad through others' eyes, and feeling enormously proud of him. It was also the first time I ate fried squid, which I found to be delicious! My horizons were expanding.

At the opening that evening, art collectors flocked into the gallery to meet Dad and to buy his art. This was a world utterly foreign to the one we inhabited in Burley, and these wealthy people were the kind of people I aspired to become when I grew up. The amazing thing in this scenario was that these people were there to meet *my dad!*

I had a hard time sleeping that night, tossing and turning as I contemplated the excitement, vitality, and energy pulsating among the glamorous art patrons. All at once, the art world was no longer to be seen in the context of a grim environment, filled with disappointment, heartache, rejection, arrogance, apathy, distress, and destitution. It was newly perceived through the clear eyes of a sixteen-year-old boy to be a sensual and vibrant scene, peopled by interesting and enchantingly exotic men and women, and brimming with the promise of fame and fortune.

MULTI-LEVEL MARKETING

Southern Idaho, like much of rural and suburban America, was rife with multi-level marketing businesses during the '80s and '90s, and for all I know, it continues to be so today. Multi-level, or pyramid marketing, appealed to a populace desperate to achieve wealth, but seeing its current jobs and income-producing prospects stalled at a dead end.

The approach of a company promoting one of these schemes was simple. For a "small" setup fee, you would start your own business, and sell the company's products. Your customers to whom you would pitch these products were your family and friends.

"Hey, these are products you are using anyway, and they're better quality, so why not help me out and buy them from me?"

After several orders, you would recruit these loyal customers to join the company for a "small investment", and they too would sell the company's products, and recruit their friends and families to join. For each new recruit, you would receive a portion of his sign-up fee and of his future sales, as would the person who recruited you, and the person who had recruited him.

A guy could make a little money by selling the products; he could make a ton of money by signing everyone he knew to join the company. "Franchise fees" or "business startup costs" could range from several hundred to several thousand dollars. If an entrepreneur proved skilled at touting the exceptional quality of the product line, and effective at recruiting through demonstrating the money to be made, he could amass a sizable fortune.

Being that they were eternal optimists and capable of running a calculator, my parents were attracted by and susceptible to these opportunistic schemes. In these instances, it seemed to them that everything they had learned about selling art would apply to selling whatever product happened to be trending at a given moment.

I specifically remember my parents signing up to sell cleaning products with one company, makeup with another, and consumer goods with the next. They gleefully signed up to sell an internet connected phone called the iPhone . . . *no, not that iPhone.* This iPhone was a telephone with a full keyboard, and a built-in black and white LCD screen; it plugged into the phone line and could dial up the internet. It was going to revolutionize the internet!

One had to be mindful to refer to these businesses as "multi-level marketing" companies, never as "pyramid marketing". Pyramid schemes were illegal, and faithful multi-level marketing adherents became quite offended were anyone to utter the word "pyramid" in their presence. To this day, I cannot understand the purported differences between the two, yet a multi-level marketing acolyte could spend hours explaining the system, and listing the inherent advantages of his company. He would also be happy to illustrate how *his product* and *your participation* could make you a millionaire.

Whenever Mom and Dad got involved with another company, a ripple of excitement passed through the family.

We would all be tucked snuggly in our beds at night, imagining what we would do with our new-found wealth.

As tight as funds were, it was surprising that Mom and Dad were so often able to put together the money to pay the sign-up fees assessed by these companies. The money spent to subsidize these rackets was sorely needed elsewhere: to cover the ongoing expenses in the sustenance of a large family.

Here lay the dilemma: could we really afford to miss out? What if this one was the Big One? Wasn't it worth taking a little risk? Making the gamble? Going for the gold?

By the time I was sixteen or seventeen, I could use a calculator myself. I argued that there was no way these businesses were sustainable.

"It doesn't make sense," I remember saying one afternoon, as I sat at the bar in the dome talking to Mom, who was fixing dinner.

"In order for one of these pyramid scams to work, you would need more people than you could possibly recruit. Take a look."

I showed her a sheet of paper, onto which I had scribbled some numbers.

"If you sign up eight people, and each of them signs up eight people," I explained, "and if each of those eight people signs up eight, and so on, this is where you end up."

1. 1 x 8 = 8
2. 8 x 8 = 64
3. 64 x 8 = 512
4. 512 x 8 = 4096
5. 4,096 x 8 = 32,768
6. 32,768 x 8 = 262,144
7. 262,144 x 8 = 2,097,152
8. 2,097,152 x 8 = 16,777,216
9. 16,777,216 x 8 = 134,217,728

10. 134,217,728 x 8 = 1,073,741,824
11. 1,073,741,824 x 8 = 8,589,834,592

"In just eleven generations of the business, you have more people signed up than there are people currently living on the planet!" I said in exasperation.

My mother replied patiently, not exhibiting the slightest irritation with my naivate.

"Well of course not everyone is going to be successful in getting eight people to sign up," she said.

"Certainly not everyone in the tenth generation," I replied. "How are you going to make money if you can't get eight people to sign up, and those eight people to sign up their own eight people?"

"I know I can get eight people registered," she said, continuing to peel potatoes.

"But what if *you* are positioned in the tenth generation?"

These conversations never went anywhere. Neither did the multi-level marketing. Mom and Dad would stick with it for a few weeks, or perhaps a month, sign a few people up, and sell a little bit of whatever merchandise the company was hawking. Soon enough, focus would shift back to Dad's painting, whereupon the company, along with our money, would fade out of sight and out of memory.

When the next inexorable opportunity came along, I reminded Mom and Dad of the last one that had flopped. They patiently explained why this new company was so much better, and how desirable its products were. They exclaimed the virtue of its founders, praised the soundness of their formula, and lauded the brilliance of their acumen.

"And," they would say as the clincher, "we're getting in very early on this one!"

RUSSIAN SPIES

One hot summer afternoon, an old Buick pulled into our driveway. It wasn't unusual for us to have unexpected visitors. From time to time, folks would pull off the highway to satisfy their curiosity and find out what the dome was all about.

The older couple who emerged from the Buick, however, spoke in thick, foreign accents when Dad stepped out onto the front deck to greet them. Mom and Dad were unfailingly hospitable, and often welcomed strangers into our house, or picked them up along the highway to give them rides. Some of the people they met in casual circumstances over the years had become lifelong friends; so it wasn't a surprise that Dad invited this couple in.

The older man and woman, it turned out, were vacuum cleaner sales reps, and asked if Mom and Dad might have a few minutes for them to demonstrate their amazing hardware. Dad agreed, and welcomed them into the dome.

I was upstairs on the third level, but could see into the living room where they laid out their wares, and could hear every word they said. I immediately noted the couple's thick accents, and was reminded of the accents of the many Russians I had heard on TV shows and in the evening news.

The couple's sales pitch was an act of futility. We had only one small patch of carpet in the home; it was in the living room, and had never been stapled down. Moreover, we already owned a perfectly serviceable vacuum that had been in the family since Mom and Dad signed up to sell vacuum cleaners to their friends and family early in their marriage.

This didn't stop the couple from showing Mom and Dad every feature of their vacuum, and demonstrating its superior sucking power.

As much as they hated to disappoint the couple, Mom and Dad stopped them half an hour into their demonstration, and politely told them that despite the exceptional quality of the vacuum cleaner, they were unable to spare the several hundred dollars to purchase it.

Oddly, even after having invested so much energy and time with their pitch, the couple didn't protest. They politely thanked my parents for their time, and packed up their gear to leave.

"This house unusuael," the wife commented, her thick accent almost incomprehensible. "You lif heer long?"

Dad replied that we had lived in the dome for a couple of years, and that he had built it himself.

"Oh, vary gud, vary gud!" the wife exclaimed, delighted with Dad's answer.

The husband thanked Dad and Mom for their time, and the two disappeared in their Buick.

It was one of the strangest encounters I had ever witnessed, and thanks to Mom and Dad's indiscriminate conviviality, I had witnessed some pretty strange interactions over the years. The more I thought about it, the more convinced I grew that selling vacuums was a ruse; the couple were clearly Russian spies. I had read enough Tom Clancy to know that this made perfect sense, if one stopped to think about it.

From satellite imagery, the dome must have seemed very odd to Russian intelligence analysts. There, set in the midst of Southern Idaho farmland, was a geodesic dome, with dimensions comparable to a radar dome. Except that it wouldn't make any logical sense to put a radar dome anywhere in the vicinity of our house. This dome must serve another purpose.

The Russians had obviously activated sleeper agents, and sent them to poke around. The agents were likely more loath to report that the dome was a residence for some crackpot capitalist artist and his obscenely large family, than they would have been to report their disappointment in failing to sell a vacuum cleaner.

Remember, there was a war on, even if it was a cold war. What might appear to the casual observer to be a trifling matter of no significance, could instead be one of sufficient magnitude to pose a threat to our national security. No one was going to pull the wool over my eyes—least of all, a Russian spy.

Saguaros in the Desert

By the early nineties, things had stabilized in our lives. Dad's career had steadily become more successful. He had consistently built up his inventory, and his artwork was now sold in a dozen or more galleries around the country. The diversity in representation, and the growing depth of his inventory, meant that sales were now coming in steadily. There were still times when our finances were tight, but the severity and length of the fiscal droughts were diminishing.

Though the dome was far from finished, we had been living in it for a few years. The financial outlay that had been required during the initial building phase had decreased significantly.

We bought a new van. We visited the Grand Canyon. We acquired a larger TV and a VCR. If not exactly signs of prosperity, these were all indicators of abating poverty.

As a further sign of our improved finances, Mom and Dad did something unexpected in the fall of 1990. After delivering artwork to a new gallery in Scottsdale, Arizona, they sat us children down in the gathering space of the dome to tell us they had an announcement to make. Mom could hardly contain her excitement.

"We've signed a lease on a house in Phoenix! We're going to move down there for the winter!"

My sisters and brothers and I sat in silence, looking to one another to determine how to respond. It was difficult to immediately grasp the implications of what she was telling us.

"Oh, and the house has a pool," she added casually, treating the most important detail of her announcement with nonchalance.

The six of us who were old enough to process the news now proceeded to lose our minds with excitement, whereupon Devon, the youngest at not yet two, broke into howling tears at all the ruckus.

"When are we leaving?"

"How big is the house?"

"How long will we be there?"

"Is it a real pool?"

We had a million questions, to which our parents both provided answers to the best of their knowledge. We could tell that they were as excited as we were. They told us we would be leaving in a few weeks' time, and thus must begin to pack.

Looking back, beyond the adventure of the move, getting out of the Idaho winters made a lot of sense from a business perspective. Dad's production during the winter typically dropped precipitously. Even though Dad was now painting in the semi-finished and heated dome, the long, cold, grey days were dismal, and invariably brought on bouts of melancholy and depression in the artist; his painting would grind to a halt, sometimes for weeks on end. Chipping the ice from the doors, dealing with dead car batteries, and listening to the howling wind proved to be more than Dad could handle for sustained lengths of time.

While there would certainly be an outlay of money to move to Arizona and to lease a home in Phoenix, Mom and

Dad hoped that they would more than make up for the expense in increased output and sales.

Mom and Dad had purchased a street atlas of Metropolitan Phoenix on their last trip to Arizona, and I spent the next several weeks poring over its pages. The atlas provided some statistics about the population, details of its geography, and information about special attractions. I was particularly excited to learn that there were many libraries in the city, the nearest being just a couple of miles from our new home. I imagined that these libraries must contain many, many more books than did our tiny Burley library. Being the nerd I was, I made Mom promise that one of the first things we would do when we got to Phoenix would be to sign me up for a library card.

The house we were renting was unfurnished, so Dad rented a large U-Haul truck. The day before our departure, we all worked to load our beds, the couches, dressers, and all of our clothing. While it was hard work, there was never a job completed with less whining and complaining than the loading of that truck. We could hardly wait to sally forth on this great adventure.

We drove as far as my grandparents' house in Utah on the first night of our trip, and the following day covered the remaining distance to Phoenix. Dad drove the U-Haul, with a couple of kids sharing the bench seat; Mom drove the the rest of the kids in the family van. Progress was slow because it was hard for Dad to get the big orange and white truck to go over fifty miles an hour. We rolled into Phoenix late in the evening.

I can still remember vividly how strange the landscape appeared, with its rock-strewn, treeless mountains, and the lonely, jutting saguaro cacti. Though it was an autumn night, when we opened the windows to get a better feel for the place, we were greeted by an intensely hot blast of desert air.

Phoenix was huge, and the city lights extended to the horizon in every direction. I had been to big cities before, but this was a different experience altogether: this big city was to be our home for the months to come.

We all piled out of the truck and van when we pulled up to the house with the distinctive southwest look on Claire Drive. The four bedroom edifice boasted two thousand square feet, and was finished in stucco. Dad unlocked the front door, and we rushed through the house, exploring the new space with excitement, and staking claim to bedrooms. I got my own room at the front of the house, the three girls chose the room next to mine, and the two younger boys took the room next to Mom and Dad's master suite.

I would soon discover that our rental property on Claire Drive was pretty typical for Phoenix. For us, however, it was pure luxury in contrast to the dome. This home had two full bathrooms, floors covered in tile and carpet, and bedrooms with real doors! Despite there being seven of us living in the house, it was plenty capacious to find a space in which one could be alone: in a bedroom, in the living room, the family room (which became Dad's studio), or outside on the expansive patio.

More importantly, from my standpoint, this house blended seamlessly with the houses surrounding it. There was nothing unusual to differentiate us from our neighbors. I loved being *normal* for a change; it was a blessed relief to fit in.

Eight months is nothing in the reckoning of time for an adult—it flies by—yet for me, an adolescent, the eight-month stretch we spent in that first house in Phoenix was a lifetime. The house became home. We made friends in the neighborhood and in our local church congregation. We progressed in our homeschool lessons. We entertained guests. And we swam, though we were likely the only ones in the metropolis swimming during the winter.

Phoenix is brutally hot during the summer, and comfortably temperate during the winter. Daily temperatures reach the hundreds through October, and the nineties into early November. For most parts of the country, that temperature range signals swimming weather. What visitors to the desert don't realize, however, is that the hot daytime temperatures of fall and spring tend to drop dramatically at night.

The nighttime cooling causes the water temperatures in Phoenix swimming pools to drop significantly. Unless their pools are heated, most Phoenicians call an end to the swimming season by the end of September.

My brothers and sisters and I enjoyed our pool far longer than was typical for the locals. Notwithstanding the icy cold water of early December, on sunny winter afternoons, we plunged into the pool and swam as long as we could stand it, which was likely three or four minutes. We then stretched out prostrate on the cooldeck to dry ourselves beneath the sun, hoping to restore the circulation of blood through our constricted veins.

True to her word, Mom got us library cards within a day or two of our arrival in Arizona, and we soon made ourselves the library's most avid subscribers. I was into science fiction by this time, and devoured books by Isaac Asimov and Carl Sagan, as well as a vast array of dime-store space operas.

I finished my school work in a couple of hours in the morning, and spent most of the afternoon and evening reading. I read over a hundred books that first winter in Phoenix.

Dad spent his days painting in the studio, or taking photos in the desert. He had a show in his Scottsdale gallery in the spring of '91. The show was a triumph, thus reaffirming the wisdom of having moved to Arizona to be closer to the gallery.

The entire winter was a success, prompting Mom and Dad to hire a realtor and to shop for a permanent second residence in Phoenix. It would prove impossible to point to any event more reflective of our altered circumstances than this hunt for real estate. No one could have foretold our imminent transformation into snowbirds.

Not five years before, we had been living in a trailer without running water. Now we were to be the proud owners of a winter home in Arizona. How fortunes had changed for the Horejs family!

LONG DAY IN THE E.R.

One weekday morning, Mom and Dad set out early with the realtor. They had been looking at houses for several days, and on this particular day they had a long list of possibilities to see.

It wasn't uncommon for my parents to leave the kids home while they were out and about. I was sixteen now, and Adrienne was a mature fourteen. The two of us were nominally in charge while my parents were gone, but everyone was doing whatever he or she chose to do. The older kids were likely working to finish school assignments or reading, and the three younger boys, including my two-and-a-half-year-old brother Devon, were playing in the backyard.

Because our rental home sat on a slight incline, the pool had been built at the highest level of the yard. A four-foot-high retaining wall separated the fenced pool from the rest of the yard, which was covered in gravel and dotted by a few shrubs.

An hour after my parents left, Yvette rushed into my room, where I had been diligently working on an algebra lesson before falling asleep on my bed (is it even conceivable to do algebra in bed and stay awake?)

"Devon fell off the wall and broke his arm!" Yvette sobbed, tears streaming down her face.

My eyes snapped open. Momentarily confused and out of place, and never a big fan of drama, I instinctually replied, "He did not!"

"Yes he did!" she insisted. "Come on!"

I twisted out of bed, and followed her through the house and out into the backyard, where Devon was sitting in the gravel screaming in pain. All of my other siblings were gathered around, trying to console their crying baby brother.

One look at the arm told me that my initial insistence that no bone had been broken, and that Yvette should remain calm, was completely misplaced. Devon's lower arm was bent at a crazy angle in a spot where there was no joint, and I immediately determined for myself what everyone else already knew to be true: *that arm was broken.*

After having spent eight years in the Cub Scouts and Boy Scouts, and having earned my first aid badge, one would think that I was well-prepared for this situation: I wasn't. It's emergencies like this that let a fellow know what he is made of; it turns out I am made of jello.

"We've got to get him to the hospital," Adrienne finally said, when it was clear I wasn't coming up with anything.

I had my license, but Mom and Dad had our family's only car, so we weren't going anywhere. Should we call 911? What would a responsible adult do? More paralysis on my part.

"Hold him still," I contributed.

"Should we call 911?" Yvette asked.

"I think we just need to take him to the emergency room," Adrienne said.

"Let's see if the neighbors will help us," Yvette suggested.

This seemed like a good idea.

"Okay," I said, "Adrienne, you stay with Devon. Yvette and I will go and see if we can get some help."

Yvette and I rushed into the house and out the front door, and ran to our neighbor's house on the right. We anxiously and repeatedly rang the bell. A woman who was known only casually to the family opened the door.

"We're sorry to bother you," I exclaimed, "but our little brother fell off our retaining wall in the backyard and broke his arm. Our parents are gone, and we're not sure when they will be back. Can you help us?"

I wish I could remember her name, or even what she looked like, because to her great credit and our eternal gratitude, our neighbor sprang into action. She called out to her husband, and the two of them sprinted back to our house with us, and into the back yard. A quick glance confirmed to our neighbors that the arm was indeed broken.

The woman instructed her husband to get his car. She wrapped Devon in a warm blanket, lifted him into my arms, and walked beside me as I carried him through the house and out to the waiting car.

"I'll stay with the younger children," our neighbor said. "Why don't the two of you go with my husband and the little one to the hospital?" she kindly urged Adrienne and me.

"Okay, thank you!" Adrienne replied as the two of us climbed into the back seat with Devon, who shrieked in agony at the slightest movement.

While enroute to the hospital, the woman's husband asked where our parents were, hoping that he could track them down. One must remember that these were the days before the widespread use of mobile phones; as soon as people left the house, they might as well have been travelling to the moon if you didn't know where they were headed, because there was no way you were going to communicate with them.

We explained that they were out with a realtor looking at houses. We had to admit we didn't know who the realtor was, or for which agency he or she worked. In other words, we knew nothing.

Devon was calm, perhaps in a state of shock, by the time we arrived at the hospital and rushed through the emergency doors. We explained to the nurse at the admissions desk what had happened, pleaded the seriousness of our emergency, and described the horrific pain our baby brother was experiencing. She glanced at his arm, and then in the manner of emergency room nurses everywhere, responded with a stack of paperwork.

"I'll need you to fill out these forms," she said, handing an admittance packet to our neighbor.

"I'm not the guardian," he quickly asserted.

"I can fill out the paperwork," I chimed in, wanting to be useful, and hoping to defuse the awkwardness.

There was some discussion about the situation with my parents; whereupon, the nurse ushered Devon and Adrienne to an examination room, while I sat in the lobby to fill out the paperwork the best I could.

Our neighbor told me he was going to go home and see whether he could do anything to locate my parents. I thanked him for getting us to the hospital, and watched him walk away. It was odd, after all of the adrenaline that had been pumping over the last twenty minutes, to now experience the anticlimax of sitting in the waiting room with the ill, the injured, and their families: all of us waiting for something to happen. Biding our time.

I handed the partially-completed paperwork to the nurse at the desk, and she glanced over it.

"We'll have to get a signature from your parents before we can do anything," she informed me.

"Isn't there something you can do for my brother while we try to find them?" I asked. "He's in a lot of pain."

"The doctor will take a look to make sure he's okay, but we really can't do anything until we have your parents' permission."

"Okay," I said, perhaps beginning to understand somewhat the frustration my parents felt with medical bureaucracy; though, I was prone to forgive it and trust that everything would turn out if we waited patiently and respectfully.

And wait we did.

Adrienne stayed with Devon in the exam room, where I checked in every half hour or so. Devon was now only occasionally crying. The pain had either diminished, or he had become accustomed to it. It wasn't long before his pain and discomfort were secondary concerns to his boredom. Devon was never one to sit still for long, and the exam room was not a very interesting place for a two-and-a-half-year-old boy to be penned.

This matter of boredom was compounded as the minutes turned into hours. I don't remember the precise time the accident occurred, nor the time we arrived at the hospital: it had happened much earlier that morning, and by noon the three of us were all tired of waiting. Unfortunately, we had no choice other than to endure this trial of our collective patience.

I must have taken my wallet, because I remember calling home on a pay phone to learn that although our neighbors hadn't had any luck finding my parents, everything was fine with our younger siblings who remained at home. I bought a couple of candy bars and sodas from the waiting room vending machine and shared them with Adrienne and Devon while we continued to wait.

Noon turned to one o'clock, and one to two. I flipped through magazines, but it was hard to concentrate on articles targeted to adults, what with all of the noise and commotion in the ER.

At some point, a social worker came and talked to us. In hindsight, I assume she was there to make certain we were not the victims of child abuse and neglect.

A doctor looked in from time to time to take Devon's temperature and to have another look at his arm.

It was late afternoon when my parents finally arrived at the hospital. Seeing them walk through the sliding glass doors of the ER filled me with a mix of intense relief and righteous fury.

"Where have you been!?" I cried, tears welling up—embarrassing for a teenager.

"We just got back," Mom said. "We just found out! Where's Devon?"

I took Mom back to the exam room, while the desk-nurse detained Dad to complete and sign the paperwork. There ensued a tear-filled reunion as Mom hugged Devon.

A few minutes later, the doctor showed up with the long awaited pain medication and a splint. I was ushered back to the waiting room while the arm was set. It wasn't long before they had a plaster cast on Devon's arm, which was held in place by a brace and bandaging. After the long and tedious hours of waiting, it seemed utterly preposterous that the doctor's work was completed so speedily.

After more paperwork, Devon was finally released, and the five of us made our way out of the hospital and into the van.

"You can never leave us that long again," I insisted with a tone of resolute determination in my voice as we pulled out of the parking lot and drove toward home.

My mother never did. In the days immediately after the accident, Mom didn't leave the house at all. In the following weeks, she initiated a routine that would continue well into my adulthood. She never stepped out the door without imparting precise information about where she was going and how to get in touch with her should the need arise. When gone for more than an hour, she called regularly to check in with us. Whenever possible, one parent remained at home. If both parents were absent, the check-ins were frequent and consistent.

It took years after the advent of cellular phones for my parents to get one; once they did, they began checking in before, during, and after long drives. To this day, Mom calls or texts someone that she and Dad are getting on the road, how long they anticipate the trip will take, and when to expect further contact.

I don't remember her being so obsessed with travel itineraries before Devon's broken arm. Nonetheless, check-ins would become a regular feature of my late-adolescence, my young-adult life, and my years as a married man. Never again was I going to have to hunt my mother down in the event of a personal or family emergency.

Guess Who's Coming to Dinner?

Sunday dinner at our house was rarely just a family affair. Often, Mom and Dad invited one of the older widows from church, or a neighbor a bit down on his luck, to join us. Mom would make a roast and potatoes or bake a chicken and her famous rolls. We would all impatiently wait to eat, with our mouths watering as the house filled with delectable aromas.

When at length the meal was set on the table, and after we offered a prayer of thanksgiving, Dad typically started a conversation with our guest, and the family would learn all about his or her life. My siblings and I thought this was pretty boring; we were annoyed that we would be expected to sit at the table until our guest and Mom and Dad were finished conversing. Sometimes these meals would drag on for hours.

Meal by meal and conversation by conversation, however, our understanding of the world and of the people in it was expanded.

Considering the many years of privation we had endured, it is now remarkable to me when I consider how generous Mom and Dad were in sharing our table. Throughout the years, I recall countless guests passing through our dining room and into our hearts.

My parents' hospitality didn't end in the dining room. Dad stopped our car on road trips to pick up hitchhikers, offering them a ride in our already crowded van. We also stopped to help folks who were having car trouble or who had run out of gas. Casual encounters would turn into lifelong friendships.

When volunteers were requested at church to help a man who had been paralyzed from the neck down in a car accident, Dad raised his hand. I would sometimes accompany him to help get the man dressed and ready for church and into a van, which had been specially modified with a ramp to load his wheelchair. We strapped his chair down with cables and ratchets and drove him to church.

When the man's medical assistants were unavailable, Dad went to his apartment in the middle of the night to take him through a series of motions that would stretch his contracted limbs and muscles. He sometimes wrangled me, or one of my siblings, into helping. Though we would whine and complain, as teenagers are wont to do, we learned compassion and the deep satisfaction that comes through giving service to those in need.

Mom was equally kind-hearted. She prepared meals to take to families who were grieving the loss of a loved one or who had just welcomed a new baby into the world. She offered to babysit children when parents were in a bind.

To this day, whenever I meet folks who have known Mom and Dad over the years they invariably comment on how kind and caring my parents were to them. "They would bend over backwards to help anyone who needed it," people say again and again. And, indeed, they would and do so still.

I Stumble into the Art World

During our second winter in Phoenix, I decided it was time to look for a job. I was in a unique position among my fellow teenagers in that I could work during the day, even during the school year, since as a homeschooler, I could complete my school assignments anytime.

Because I loved books so much, I first put in job applications at all of the local bookstores. This was the early '90s, so there were still many bookstores in business. I also applied for a number of jobs in hotels and retail shops. I really didn't care much where I worked, as long as I had something steady. I was interested in supplementing the income I was earning from building Dad's canvases, because I wanted to save enough money to buy a car.

While dropping off an application at a bookstore that was looking to hire a manager (oh yes, some of my parents' optimism was rubbing off!), I locked my keys in the car. I called home to let Dad know, but there wasn't much he could do about it: though we now had two cars, Mom had the second car at the Scottsdale gallery that was representing Dad's work. The gallery had recently expanded, and Mom had agreed to work for the owners for a few weeks while they looked to expand their staff. Dad called her at the gallery and shared the details of my dilemma.

Before leaving work on her rescue mission, she explained to the owner of the gallery that I had been out applying for a job when I locked my keys in the car. Despite this silly demonstration of incompetence on my part, he told my mom that if I was interested in working part time in the gallery, he would hire me to help in the backroom.

When offered the job, I accepted without hesitation. In retrospect, I wonder at my enthusiasm to willingly step into the art industry. Hadn't my father's vocation engendered years of privation, discouragement, and chaos, robbing me of the security, stability, and normalcy I so deeply craved? By pure happenstance, I was launched into my own career in art.

Whatever was I thinking?

Hey, I was seventeen years old and hallelujah happy to have a job.

Almost Famous

Mom and Dad did find a home to purchase in Phoenix. They bought a four bedroom out of foreclosure, not too far from the house we had rented that first year in Phoenix. This one sat across the street from a large city park and a few short blocks from the mountain preserves. The preserves are lands maintained and protected by the city and comprise hundreds of miles of trails that wind through rocky hills and small mountains right in the middle of Phoenix. The house had a large family room above the garage that would prove to be the perfect studio space for Dad.

This was an amazing set-up for Dad; he needed to concentrate on his painting. By this point, he was reaching the zenith of his mid-career. He was showing in major galleries in Scottsdale, Arizona; Santa Fe, New Mexico; Palm Desert, California; Boise and Sun Valley, Idaho; Portland, Oregon; Jackson Hole, Wyoming; Naples and Sarasota, Florida; and Alexandria, Virginia. These galleries were achieving steady sales, and his work was being acquired by collectors from around the country and throughout the world.

My parents had achieved something remarkable in building Dad's career. They had taken him from being a completely unknown, unrepresented artist, and in ten years (the roller coaster years) had established John Horejs as a nationally recognized, financially successful, and highly revered artist.

Day by day, Dad had honed his artistic skill, and Mom had sharpened her marketing acumen. The two of them had persistently built contacts and relationships, both in galleries and in the broader art market. They had been fearless in consistently striking out to cold-call new galleries to seek representation.

The sacrifices we had all made, and the lessons we had learned during the difficult early years, were beginning to pay off. As a family, we felt grateful for our hard-won success, and the sense of security it engendered.

Some of the habits we adopted during the lean years stayed with us, even as our finances stabilized. We were still frugal in our spending, except in the immediate afterglow of a huge sale, at which time we might drop some cash on a new car, a fancy television, or a family vacation.

I was now reaching late adolescence and old enough to appreciate the difference financial stability brought to our lives. There were still some dry spells when the inherent instability of the art market would lead to a patch without any sales, but the frequency and severity of those lean times declined dramatically. My younger siblings were growing up in an altogether different financial landscape than did their older brother and sisters.

The future was looking bright, and there was no reason to believe that the upward trend in Dad's career would not continue.

Unfortunately, my parents were about to take a major detour, a detour that would change all of our lives.

Shadow Revolution

Even as our financial situation grew steadily brighter, Mom and Dad were entangling themselves in a perilous scheme. Unlike the multi-level marketing businesses, which had been expensive yet ultimately harmless, this undertaking would very nearly destroy our family.

As Dad's career flourished, and as the money began to roll in, it came to be bitterly difficult for Mom and Dad to pay taxes on their income. It must have been dismaying to write such large checks to the Treasury Department. Unlike regular wage earners, who had their taxes invisibly and routinely deducted from their paychecks, my parents had to draft sizable checks to pay their taxes and then watch the money they felt was theirs disappear into the vaults of the federal government.

The amount they were paying in taxes surpassed the amount they had made in total during those arduous early years. Not only was the government taking a considerable chunk of their hard-earned money, it was spending it on programs my parents did not support.

Although no one likes to pay taxes, my parents were primed to resent taxes even more than most. The seeds of their anti-government sentiment, which had been planted by their friends in Idaho, had taken root, and were now beginning to blossom in Phoenix. They met others in our church congregation in Phoenix, who like they, were anti-government and anti-tax. These friends were affiliated with loosely organized "patriot" groups, wherein members shared stories about the injustices and conspiracies that were being fostered by the federal government.

There were stories about how the Sixteenth Amendment, the amendment authorizing the federal collection of an income tax, had never been properly ratified. They talked about how the IRS was abusing its police powers to harass law-abiding citizens to extort money from them. There were accounts of patriots who were standing up to federal authorities and refusing to comply with purportedly unconstitutional tax laws, as well as with other overreaches by the feds.

Then, of course, there were the blatant examples of government violence against citizens at Ruby Ridge and Waco.

I overheard conversations about the growing resistance to the government when Mom and Dad invited anti-government friends to our home to join them in railing against The System.

Mom and Dad occasionally tried to talk to my siblings and me about what they were learning and thinking about the government. My sisters seemed mostly uninterested; however, they were somewhat frightened by the talk of heavily armed U.S. Treasury agents breaking down doors and arresting entire families. I was openly hostile to any such conversation.

In my wide-ranging reading over the years, I had invested many hours in the biographies of presidents, non-fictional accounts of government agencies, and spy and war novels. I had also developed an addiction to watching the evening news, a side effect of having only one television station to choose from in Idaho.

Somehow, in all that reading and watching, I found myself fascinated by the government and by the political process. I felt as though I understood what was going on in Washington. What my parents were telling us about massive conspiracies devised to oppress the American people simply didn't match what I was seeing. I couldn't believe these revolutionary plots could remain hidden from the press or that the press must somehow be complicit with their perpetrators.

It's probably fair to say that I was fully in the throws of adolescence and likely would have rebelled against anything my parents tried to tell me. Unlike rebels of the sixties and seventies, I found myself trying to convince my parents that the establishment wasn't the enemy: their anti-government friends were.

I had no power to sway Mom and Dad, however, as they had already withdrawn from a number of the conventions of the day. All of their seven kids were now being home-schooled. Cameron, Graydon, and Devon, the youngest three at the time, would never see the inside of a public-school classroom. My parents had chosen not to register my brothers for social security numbers and not to have them vaccinated.

Though we were now spending more time living a somewhat conventional lifestyle in Phoenix, it was all appearances. Slowly but surely, Mom and Dad were withdrawing from more and more of the conventions and norms of contemporary American life.

In 1994, at the age of nineteen, I escaped the burgeoning tension brought on by my parents' anger at the government when, despite my earlier hostility to religious thought, I volunteered to serve for two years as a Mormon missionary in Sao Paulo, Brazil. Over the years, I had come to see that my parents' unconventional views of life, together with their approach to raising us outside the system, had nothing whatever to do with our faith. I had become good friends with a number of the members of the congregation, including scout and youth group leaders, who had helped me adopt a more moderate view of religion that culminated in my decision to become a missionary.

Many readers who have seen young Mormon missionaries in their white shirts and ties will find it interesting to learn that, not only do Mormon missionaries serve their missions without any kind of remuneration, they actually pay all their own expenses, including travel, housing, and food.

I hadn't saved much of the money I had earned over the years working to build Dad's stretchers; nor had I set aside much of anything the year I worked in the Scottsdale gallery. Thus, Mom and Dad of necessity had to help me pay for my missionary expenses. This they did without complaint.

Though this was my first experience living unsupervised and away from my family, I found that I was well prepared. My parents had given me and my sisters and brothers autonomy and responsibility throughout our childhoods. I didn't find the impoverished conditions I encountered in some of the areas where I lived in Brazil much different from the circumstances in which I had been raised. As it turned out, my childhood had suited me well for thriving in the third world!

I happily discovered that I had the same facility Dad exhibited in picking up the Portuguese language. I, too, loved the people I met and served in Brazil. It sweetened the experience to know that I was living an adventure in a culture that had resonated with my father so many years before.

Throughout my time in the Southern Hemisphere, I corresponded by letter with my family. Mom wrote frequently, was always cheerful, and shared upbeat news from the family. Dad, never much for writing, sent an occasional note, or told Mom to convey his greetings. There was no mention of their ongoing effort to fight the government, and, before long, I was so caught up in my new life as a missionary that I began to forget about it.

When I returned from Brazil to Phoenix in February of 1996, however, I was struck by how much older both of my parents now appeared—especially my father. At the time, I thought it was just the effect of not having seen them for two years; I would later come to believe that the growing stress of their posturing against the government had aged them prematurely.

About this time, my parents took the next major step forward in their battle against the government: they stopped filing their income tax returns. They had spent hundreds of hours reading tax law and legal theory written by both government and anti-government lawyers. Among other assertions, my parents claimed that they were citizens of the State of Idaho, not of the United States, and, therefore, did not owe federal income tax. They staked their freedom and their financial future on this claim, and, by default, they wagered the future of the entire Horejs family on the bet.

It seemed like a sucker's bet to me.

Romantic Interlude

After returning from Brazil, I went back to work in the Scottsdale gallery where I had been hired prior to serving my mission. I was now working full time and started seriously thinking about what I would do with my life.

I knew that I wanted to go to college. When I asked Mom and Dad about funding for higher education, I learned that they didn't have the money to help pay for it. In the thick of raising seven kids, owning two homes, and fighting the government, their funds, understandably, were tightly stretched.

I realized I would have to work to pay my way through school. I also knew that I wanted to get out on my own as soon as I could.

In 1996, the owners of the Scottsdale gallery invited me to work for the summer in their Jackson Hole, Wyoming gallery, and I eagerly accepted. They agreed to rent an apartment for me through the summer, and in return, I would work six days a week in the gallery.

Soon before I left for Wyoming, I met Carrie Williams, the daughter of a prominent Phoenix attorney. The family were members of our local church congregation. Carrie had been away at school, and returned to Phoenix in early May to work a summer job and be with her family. We met through a mutual friend, and I was immediately smitten by her beauty and her poise.

One Sunday, Carrie was standing with her mom, Karly, in the hallway of the church after Sunday services. As I walked by, Karly grabbed me, and started a conversation. She mentioned that she and her husband, Daryl, had just seen an exciting action movie and suggested that Carrie and I ought to go see it together. I readily assented, and Carrie and I scheduled a day and time to see the film.

After seeing the movie, Carrie and I talked late into the night, and, over the next several weeks, we managed to see each other frequently. We had only a short time to get to know each other before I was to leave for Wyoming, and we made the most of it.

I learned about her interests, and about her childhood and family, and she learned a bit and tad about my background—or at least its outlines. There were details I felt I couldn't tell her about my family's circumstances; as the daughter of an attorney, Carrie had grown up in conditions totally unlike those I had known. I was mortified at the possibility she might learn about the poverty I had experienced as a child. I was far more forthcoming in sharing my ambitions for the future than in recounting the details of my impoverished past. I was afraid my humble beginnings might scare her away, and therefore tried to compensate with big talk about projected prospects.

I was falling in love, and it appeared Carrie was too, yet I feared our relationship was destined to fizzle when I left for Wyoming at the end of May. Carrie would be back in school when I returned in the fall. It seemed to me we would never see one another again, at least not in time for it to matter.

Thank goodness fate had other plans. It happened that Carrie's grandfather lived in Star Valley, Wyoming, just an hour south of Jackson, where I would be working. She would be visiting for a week in July, and we made plans to see one another then. We also nonchalantly made plans to write: we were both playing it cool.

I still have copies of the letters we exchanged during that first summer, and I treasure my memories of Carrie's visit to Wyoming. They say that distance makes the heart grow fonder, though I tend to believe that it's more likely to make it wander. Happily, the former assertion proved to be true for us. We transitioned from writing to conversing on the phone, running up hundreds of dollars in bills. We saw each other whenever we could. I stopped to see her at school in Provo, Utah, on my way back to Phoenix in the fall. She came home for the holidays.

My life soon revolved around when I would next talk to Carrie, and I counted the days until I would see her next. Over the course of hundreds of phone calls, letters, and new-fangled emails, we came to know one another better, and our mutual love grew deeper.

In October of 1997, I asked Carrie to marry me. We were wed in May of 1998.

I felt I knew every detail of Carrie's life, and understood how she viewed the world. I'm sure she imagined she knew and understood the same about me. The truth of the matter was that I still had a few revelations to make: I just needed to find the right time and opportunity . . .

The Wheels of Justice Turn Slowly

Mom was crying as she spoke. My heart was pounding, and I felt blood rushing to my head and flushing my face.

I sat alone in our basement apartment in Springville, cradling the phone and trying to figure out what to say.

"I don't see how you aren't going to end up in jail," I finally said, hoping the double negative might somehow soften the blow.

Mom had just told me that the IRS had conducted raids on several of the galleries where Dad was showing his work, and had seized thousands of dollars worth of paintings. The art was to be auctioned off to collect money the IRS calculated was owed in back taxes. A criminal investigation had been opened, and more action was likely forthcoming.

Mom wanted me to hear about what had happened from her, not from a sibling or from anyone else.

"I don't want to see you end up in prison," I repeated, after several moments of silence.

"We believe in what we're doing," Mom replied, choking on the words. "We don't believe they have the right to take our money."

"I don't think they care what you believe."

Dad and I had already hashed this out many times. He had what he felt was a rock solid case against the government. He explained that our inalienable rights to life, liberty, and property, meant that the government could not put him in jail, because they would be violating two of those rights.

I argued that there were plenty of people sitting in jail for tax evasion. He countered that he and Mom were not evading taxes. He sought to justify their stance through his reasoning that if they didn't owe the government any of their earnings, they legally didn't owe taxes.

"If you look at all of the cases," he argued, "you'll see that they send people to jail for something other than the taxes. Perjury, collusion, conspiracy—but never for taxes."

"And you think they won't send you to prison on similar charges?" I asked.

"We're being exceedingly careful not to give them grounds."

Some variation of this conversation occurred on dozens of occasions, both before Dad and Mom stopped filing their taxes and after. I found it exasperating because the outcome seemed so clear. Nonetheless, my parents were adamant in their rectitude.

"I have to do this," Dad would say. "I have to do it for you and for your kids. We must start a revolution to free us from the oppression of the government."

"I don't want you to do it for me! Even if you are right," I would argue, "and I'm not saying you are—but even if you are, and even if the income tax system is unconstitutional, do you think they're going to stop? If you somehow managed to prove the law invalid, they would simply write another law. There's nothing certain in this life except death and taxes. You can't change that!"

"I believe we can."

"I believe you're going to go to prison."

"I promise you we're not going to go to prison."

"That's a promise you can't keep."

I met Carrie on a shady part of campus, and we sat together on a bench.

"There's something I need to tell you about my parents," I said.

I told her about my mother's phone call, and the seizure of artwork. I explained the long history of my parents' anti-government sentiment. I was nervous about how Carrie would respond, but other than being shocked and mystified by her new in-laws' activity, she appeared to take the whole thing in stride.

We were still very much in the honeymoon phase of our marriage, and were far enough removed from my family to be intently focused on building our own lives together. While the situation was disturbing, we couldn't think what to do about it, and saw no benefit in dwelling on it.

For a long time, Mom and Dad did not go to jail. Once the artwork had been seized, the case settled into the slow grind of government bureaucracy and legal procedure. My parents filed pro se motions to have their artwork returned, but lost every motion. The artwork was auctioned off.

The seizures had initially resulted in a public relations nightmare for their galleries, and a humiliation for Mom and Dad. No gallery owner wants customers to see IRS agents carrying artwork out of their establishment. Dad persisted in his painting, nevertheless, and resupplied the galleries with new artwork. Life proceeded much as it had before, excepting there was now a giant black cloud looming over the family's future.

I was particularly concerned about what would happen to my younger siblings who were still living at home. There was a passel of them!

My sister Marnae, child number eight, had been born while I was away on my mission in Brazil. Mom had recently given birth to her ninth and final child, Braxton, shortly before Carrie and I were married. I was twenty-four at the time, nearly a generation older than my youngest sibling! I wish I could say that I was beyond the embarrassment of having come from a large family, but it was somewhat awkward at our wedding party when my mom had to leave our reception line to nurse my baby brother.

As the government's case against my parents proceeded, Adrienne and I talked about what would become of our younger siblings if Mom and Dad were to be imprisoned. We spoke with Grandma and Grandpa Summers, who let us know they were planning to take in as many of the kids as they could if that were to happen.

I believed that the tension and stress of the ongoing battle were inflicting emotional scars on my younger brothers and sisters, yet I felt powerless to stop what was transpiring. Mom and Dad remained steadfast in their resolution to hold the line.

The legal process dragged on and on through the early years of my marriage. Carrie graduated from college, and we had our first child, a daughter. We were now fully engaged in our own lives, and my parents' legal troubles factored less and less into our daily concerns.

In 2001, Carrie and I decided to do something that would have been completely shocking to my younger self—we opened our own art gallery in Scottsdale. We called the gallery Xanadu, and represented a number of different artists from around the country. Some of these artists I had met while working in the gallery business, while others were acquaintances of my parents. First and foremost, I represented my father.

To say that our early days owning our gallery were difficult would be an understatement. Our first day of business was September 11th, 2001, and the recession that followed the terrorist attacks of that day had a devastating impact on the art market. It took years for the market to recover, and not long after it did, the country was hit with the Great Recession that reared its ugly head in December of 2007.

Our dreams of building a successful gallery business proved ever more difficult to achieve. The story of the eventual growth of our business and our struggles to overcome the challenges are part of a different story, one that I will tell when I know how it all turns out. Suffice it to say, things were hard for us in those early years, but they were even worse for my parents.

In addition to their art sales slowing because of economic circumstances, the IRS continued to build its case throughout the early 2000s, and to put pressure on Mom and Dad. Treasury agents sent notices, served motions, and filed liens against my parents' homes in Idaho and Arizona, against their vehicles, and against their artwork.

I learned from my sisters and brothers who were still living at home that the tension was building to a breaking point. Dad had a hard time focusing on his painting, which further slowed sales, creating a vicious cycle. His temper was short, and the tendency to blow up that had been a regular feature of my childhood, was re-emerging.

Dad was still convinced that once they got to court, their case would be dismissed. He confided in me that he thought his case might be the catalyst for changing the government forever, and for abolishing the IRS.

I continued to think that he was going to end up in jail.

In 2005, I received a notice from the IRS requesting that I share records of Dad's sales through our gallery over the last few years. This was my first direct involvement in the case, and I was not excited by the prospect of somehow becoming entangled in the proceedings.

I told Mom about the notice, and she advised me that I didn't need to share anything with the IRS unless they issued a subpoena. I talked to my lawyer, and he suggested it would be wise to comply with the request. I listened to my lawyer, and followed his counsel. I could now identify to some degree what it felt like to be an informant. I didn't like the feeling.

The IRS finally put the case before a grand jury in 2005. In December, an indictment came down, charging Mom and Dad with obstructing the "due administration of the internal revenue laws", with filing false trusts, and with failing to file income tax returns.

I was following the case online, and felt sick as I read that they were facing up to five years in prison and $250,000 in fines. Suddenly, the interminable wait, and the endless worry about the outcome of my parents' actions, was coming to a head. I could not have been less happy that my predictions of prison time were likely coming true.

Dad remained optimistic; their court appointed attorney was less confident. He advised Mom and Dad that prison time was not only a possibility, but an inevitability if they persisted in waging war. His advice was to stop fighting, plead guilty, and ask the judge for leniency.

I know that the decision was very difficult. Mom and Dad had invested years in their battle against the government: they had staked their reputations and their financial security on the merits of their quest. They had friends who were encouraging them to stand tough. On the other hand, they finally acknowledged the inexorable truth of what they stood to lose if they fought through to the end. The whole situation was excruciatingly distressing, especially now that an actual court date had been set.

First Mom, and then Dad, came to accept their lawyer's advice. A guilty plea was entered, saving both the government and my parents the inconvenience and expense of lengthy litigation. The judge set a date for sentencing.

Again heeding their lawyer's guidance, Mom and Dad solicited their family and friends to write letters to the judge, extolling my parents' virtues.

One hundred and seventy-eight letters were written.

Over the years, my Mom and Dad touched many lives. It was easy for me, especially during the last years of their fight with the government, to get caught up in thinking my parents had somehow gone insane—to forget all of the good that they had done in my life, in the lives of my brothers and sisters, our extended family and friends, and perhaps most telling, in the lives of strangers.

Letters poured in addressed to the judge who was in charge of sentencing. During the sentencing hearing, he said that he had never seen so many letters and that those letters were a contributing factor in his display of leniency in setting forth the terms for punishment.

His Honor, the judge, noted that my parents had admitted their guilt and expressed remorse. He referenced the lofty character witnessed in the letters. He commented on the fact that Mom and Dad had five children living at home, two of them preschoolers. He handed down a sentence that was sprinkled with mercy and lighter than what the prosecution had recommended. He sentenced Dad to six months in prison, after which he would serve a year of supervised detention. Mom received no jail time: she was sentenced instead to serve six months of supervised home detention, followed by five years of probation.

Dad was to serve his time in Safford, Arizona, and Mom would conduct her supervised detention in their Phoenix home, where she would be required to wear an electronic ankle monitor. The ankle monitor would enable Mom to make scheduled visits to Dad in prison, as her every move could be tracked by the authorities.

The terms of the probation required my parents to make timely tax filings, which would be overseen by the court and audited by the IRS each year. The judge reasoned that five years of the dutiful payment of taxes should be an effective means to reform their errant tax behavior.

The concluding penalty was that Mom and Dad were to settle all of their past due taxes and penalties with the IRS. His Honor strongly admonished them to never repeat this disgraceful lapse in fulfilling their civic obligations.

I felt no pleasure in having been proven right in my predictions of jail time. I was truly thankful that the sentences hadn't been more severe. I hoped that my letter to the judge played some small part in moving him to leniency. Perhaps my pleas for mercy on behalf of my parents somehow counterbalanced my earlier cooperation with the IRS.

Mom and Dad drove back to Phoenix from Idaho, where the sentencing had taken place, and then to Safford, where Dad surrendered himself at the federal prison to serve his sentence.

By this time, there were a number of young grandchildren in the family. Carrie and I had two children, with a third on the way, and Adrienne, Yvette, and Shalece were also married and mothers of several children each. Our daughter, Mikell, was the oldest, at six years of age, and it seemed unlikely that she and the other, younger grandchildren comprehended what was happening to their grandparents.

Mom requested that we not tell the children that their grandfather was in jail, but rather that he was away for a while. The children all seemed to accept his absence without question; after all, Mom and Dad were still traveling back and forth between Idaho and Arizona, so his being away was nothing unusual. This didn't mean they didn't miss their grandpa; on the contrary, they dearly loved the man who was affectionately known as "the tickle monster".

LIFE

My heart was pounding as we walked through the front door. Mom had invited our family over for dinner to celebrate Dad's return. I was surprised to find myself nervous at the prospect of seeing my father.

He and I had argued so much over the years, and now that he had returned from prison, I didn't know how our relationship would stand. Would he resent me, or think me smug for having been proven right about prison?

My kids rushed into the house and down the steps that led from the entryway into the kitchen and dining room.

"Grandpa, grandpa!" they shouted with delight, as they saw Dad, who was waiting to greet them.

He grabbed each of them into his arms in big, long hugs.

"Hi Dad," I said as I reached him.

"Hello, Jason," he said as he put down a child and pulled me into an embrace.

"I've missed you," I said, tears falling onto my cheeks.

"Me too," he replied in a half-whisper.

A good story should have a beginning, a middle, and an end. I guess this story ends with that embrace.

It didn't surprise me at all to learn that Dad had turned his prison experience into a positive one. He had made a variety of friends while serving his time, and many had come to look to him for encouragement because of his positive attitude.

There were still challenges to face when he was released. He and Mom had to sell their Phoenix house to satisfy the back taxes, penalties, and interest owed to the Treasury Department. When all those debts were settled, together with other debts that had accumulated during their war with the IRS, there was a little money left, which allowed them to get into a new home.

Though Mom and Dad still had misgivings about how the government was run, the fight seemed to have gone out of them, and Dad was able to turn his focus to his painting. He was intent upon making his career a top priority, after having been sidetracked by a plethora of extraneous concerns.

Even though I was in my late twenties, a business owner, and a married father of three children, it wasn't until then that I truly felt like an independent adult. I had struck out on my own nearly a decade earlier; nonetheless, it wasn't until we embraced, and I felt his love for me and my love for him that I knew something had changed.

Dad wasn't diminished in any way from his time in prison, yet I felt that I had grown somehow. It wasn't that we were equals: Dad had experienced so much more than I, but I had come to realize that my life was my own, and that its shape and direction were mine alone to make. I was no longer tethered to my parents' decisions, philosophies, or outlooks on life.

That didn't mean I could or wanted to escape their influence. To a large extent, everything we are is the sum total of what our parents have made of us. Much of what is good or bad in our natures can be traced back to the experiences we shared with our parents, their responses to the vicissitudes of daily living, and the attitudes they demonstrated during our youth. I can both credit and blame my parents, particularly my father, for the man I am today.

I suffer from a dread of car trouble, for example, and am prone to curse at the slightest hint of an engine sputter. I loathe home-improvement projects, but I can paint, hammer, sand, and saw with facility. I chronically and patently underestimate how long any project is going to take.

I have a healthy fear of the tax man, and take tax deductions with more than a modicum of caution.

I feel physically ill when someone invites me to hear a pitch for a multi-level marketing opportunity. I never accept such an invitation.

I love art. I love selling art. I love immersing myself in art.

I'm not afraid to take risks, and love owning my own business.

I love meeting new people, and I've never been afraid to start a conversation with a stranger, whether she be the CEO of an international company or he be a man living in the streets.

Everything I am I owe to my parents.

I remember distinctly thinking as a small child that I was a very lucky kid and that I wouldn't trade my parents for any other parents in the world. I still feel that way today.

The reader will note that I have spoken of my parents in the past tense in this book, as if they were no longer with us. This is not the case. As I write this memoir, Dad, now 70, is actively pursuing his painting career, creating the finest work he has ever produced; Mom is managing Dad's career, and is working as my gallery director. I'm lucky to be able to represent Dad in my gallery and to sell his work. I'm directly benefiting from Mom's incomparable sales expertise, garnered from her years of entrepreneurial endeavors.

A book like this, one that lets skeletons out of the closets of the past, probably shouldn't be written while its protagonists are still alive to feel the discomfort of having their history laid out for the world to examine. I hope, however, that writing now allows me to see the past more clearly. I hope, too, that it gives my parents the opportunity to rebut anything they feel is inaccurate.

Before you judge my parents too harshly for the unconventional life they lead, and for the challenging situations to which they subjected us all, I should let you know that there is not a thing I would change about my parents, or about my past.

I also invite you to imagine what your children, if you have children, might say regarding you, were they to write a book about their childhood. I suspect every family has its skeletons and that every parent tilts at windmills. My parents just did it all with more gusto and style.

I should also note that this book is not my entire life story. I like to think that I have many years and adventures ahead. I might have more to say about my life in the future, perhaps concerning the challenges Carrie and I faced as we opened Xanadu Gallery, and worked to see it grow and evolve.

There might also be some stories that only my children can tell.

Hopefully after I'm dead . . .

EPILOGUE

In 2017, my brother Devon (the reader will remember his broken arm) moved from Vancouver, Washington, back to Burley, to live in the dome where he had been born thirty years earlier.

A talented musician, Devon decided that the still-unfinished dome would make a perfect recording studio. He immediately set about cleaning up the property, removing decades' worth of detritus, cobwebs, and dust that had accumulated in his absence.

When Devon commenced his work, he picked up a dream that had begun forty years before. The cherished aspiration of his parents now became a multi-generational ambition.

He plans to finish the project in a few months' time . . .

DID MY FAMILY'S STORY RESONATE WITH YOU?

Thank you, dear reader, for allowing me to share my family's story. This volume has been a labor of love for me, and before you set it aside, I invite you to undertake two small tasks of your own.

First, take a look at my father's artwork on my gallery's website, www.xanadugallery.com. If you haven't yet seen his work in a gallery, you will instantly appreciate his artistic genius. Who knows, you may even find that you want to add a John Horejs painting to your collection! I would be happy to help you make that happen!

Second, if my story resonated with you, please take a moment to email me and share your thoughts about this book. Possibly you have a parent who had a creative approach to life, or maybe you have inflicted your own brand of creativity upon your loved ones. Perhaps you have led a perfectly normal life, one that would have made me envious in my youth. Whatever the case, I would be delighted to hear your reaction to my upbringing. Email me at jason@xanadugallery.com.

49947215R00096

Made in the USA
Middletown, DE
23 June 2019